PRAISE FOR SMOOTH SAILING

This book can be your best friend in the early stages of business development. Cheri offers wise, concise, and conversational counsel to make what can be confusing easy to understand and apply. With *Smooth Sailing* as your guide, you'll be empowered to ask the right questions and make critical decisions that will turn your dreams into your future. You put your heart and soul into your business, so do it right legally. It's easy to play naive and procrastinate on important legal matters, while you focus on what feels fun and urgent. If you make sound decisions up front, you'll not only enjoy peace of mind knowing you are legally protected, you'll also build a foundation for productivity and profitability.

— STACY JULIAN, AUTHOR, BLOGGER, PODCASTER,
TEACHER, BUSINESS OWNER

I have coached countless entrepreneurs throughout the years and can say with great certainty that most of them do not have the appropriate legal protections around their businesses. That's why I am thrilled that Cheri Andrews has written her book, *Smooth Sailing: A Practical Guide to Legally Protecting Your Business*. This book is packed with practical tips, and Cheri's writing style is approachable and understandable (no legalese here!). If you own a business, here's the next book you should buy!

— JILL CELESTE, AUTHOR, *THAT FIRST CLIENT*, AND
FOUNDER, CELESTIAL UNIVERSITY

Smooth Sailing: A Practical Guide to Legally Protecting Your Business is the perfect resource to help small business owners, solopreneurs, and entrepreneurs to better understand the legalities of their businesses. Business owners wear many hats as they build, grow, and maintain their businesses. Having a legally sound business is just one of the important facets that needs to be attended to in order to be safe and protected. Do yourself a favor and get yourself a copy of Cheri's book so that you can educate yourself about what your particular business needs.

Smooth Sailing by Cheri Andrews provides clear and essential guidance for those of us who have embarked on the voyage of entrepreneurship. With Cheri's guidance, I discovered a framework for navigating legal and tax decisions to support my business as it grows. Thanks, Cheri!

Packed with actionable advice for **ending small business failure**! In *Smooth Sailing: A Practical Guide to Legally Protecting Your Business*, Cheri Andrews delves into the activity of running a small business—such business formation, contracts, and website policies along with step-by-step guidance to ensure your email marketing is legally compliant. This is a much-needed resource for all small business owners!

Many first-time entrepreneurs struggle when it comes to setting up their business entity. *Smooth Sailing: A Practical Guide to Protecting Your Business* is an excellent resource to help readers easily understand the different types of business entities. Cheri Andrews explains the advantages, tax treatments, and disadvantages of each in layman's terms. Make sure you launch your new business on solid ground with the helpful information found in the pages of this book.

— TAMMI GRANT, CEO, TRAVELWHIRLED

Every small business owner should read this book—the earlier in their business journey the better! Cheri Andrews breaks down the key areas that every business owner needs from a legal perspective. I wish I had this book many years ago when I started out. Give yourself a gift and read this book to arm yourself with the knowledge so you can thrive without experiencing legal headaches and pitfalls that come from blissful ignorance or trying to DIY legal advice.

— PAULA GREGOROWICZ, OWNER,
THE PAULA G COMPANY, LLC

Legal documents and advice can often be confusing and mind-numbing. Cheri Andrews walks you step-by-step through the most common legal documents and compliance issues important to small business owners and explains what is needed and why, and when you need to consult with specific professionals. This is a great reference book to help ensure that you have everything in place to legally protect yourself and your business.

— JUDY KANE, FOUNDER, ALIGNED CONSCIOUSNESS

Cheri Andrews is a brilliant, approachable business attorney with a servant's heart. Her book *Smooth Sailing* is an easy-to-read, practical guide that walks entrepreneurs through the legal process of business ownership and best business practices. Read this book to clearly understand how you can protect yourself and your business. I would not set sail without Cheri Andrews on my ship!

— KAMIE LEHMANN, PODCAST HOST OF
SHE'S INVINCIBLE

Cheri Andrews really hits home with her overview of business structures. Her clear explanation of each type of structure allows the reader to envision their own business and the risk assessment to consider for their individual situation. Picturing the business structure as a boat helps the reader to value the importance of this decision. After all, the contents of the boat won't make it to the destination without a solid ability to float!

— CLARISSA MAKHOUL, PARTNER,
MAKHOUL FINANCIAL SERVICES

Cheri Andrews takes the "yuck" out of legal. (Okay...there is no 'yuck' in legal, but I know you know what I mean.) Cheri uses language that is easily understood and simple to digest. Her book is now included in my new bookkeeping client welcome package. Whether your business is brand new or established, her legal checklist will help you to know whether or not your business is legally compliant.

— CONNIE JO MILLER, OWNER,
ENIGMA BOOKKEEPING SOLUTIONS

Smooth Sailing is a must-read for any small business owner who has avoided the legal stuff, thinking it could wait for when her business got bigger. This easy-to-read guide will teach you what you must deal with right away and what truly can wait for later.

— SUZANNE TREGENZA MOORE,
BUSINESS & MARKETING COACH

Cheri Andrews has written the most concise, usable, practical guide to legally starting, running, and growing your business. The best part? It's in plain English and the advice is spot-on. I easily recognized a half dozen mistakes and oversights that cost me plenty in the first few years of my entrepreneurial journey. Read this book—use this book—and your small business won't stay small for very long!

— DAVID NEWMAN, AUTHOR OF *DO IT! MARKETING*

In the introduction of *Smooth Sailing*, Cheri Andrews asks several pointed questions about the course you are on as a business owner. I shook my head "YES "as I read each question out loud. At that moment, I knew I needed to read *Smooth Sailing* from cover to cover. And I know you will too!

— JENNIFER NICHOLS, OWNER, BLOOM AND HUSTLE

Cheri Andrews uses plain English to give helpful advice for starting a new business. This is a "must-read" for anyone with a business idea!

— SARAH POPOVICH, FINANCIAL ADVISOR,
MERRILL LYNCH

I never thought that I would be excited to read a legal book! *Smooth Sailing* helped me understand how important it is for business owners to have a lawyer on their team. If you are a start-up business and you want your business to be legally protected, this book is a great tool to empower you to feel confident when you consult with a lawyer.

— MAJET REYES, BUSINESS OWNER, DIVAGIRL

What a great resource tool for those who are starting a business or contemplating doing so! There is little forgiveness for not knowing or understanding legal ramifications in the business world. This book addresses the foundation on which your business will ultimately stand. Cheri Andrews, Esq., takes the reader on a journey of those requirements in an easy-to-understand manner while minimizing overwhelm. To better enable any new business owner to excel at service to their clients or customers, get this part right first!

— DONNA J. SPINA, PCC CPC ELI-MP,
BUSINESS BUILDER ACCELERATOR

While entrepreneurship is grandiose, the 'ship' must be sturdy enough to weather all the conditions that the owner will face in the course of launching and running their business. *Smooth Sailing: A Practical Guide to Legally Protecting Your Business* is the business owner's guide to building a strong and sturdy ship. While I am among the many small business owners who just wanted to get down to the good work of delivering my services, I learned—sometimes the hard way—that every business, no matter the size, must be legally protected. In this book, Andrews lays out what having a legally safe business entails in a way that is accessible, clear, and removes the intimidation factor. Whether you are just launching your business, or you have already set sail, this is a must read to ensure that the foundation of your business will sustain you over time.

— ADINA B. TOVELL, MBA, M.ED., CPC,
COURAGE TO BE CURIOUS, LLC

SMOOTH SAILING

SMOOTH SAILING

A PRACTICAL GUIDE TO
LEGALLY PROTECTING YOUR BUSINESS

CHERI D. ANDREWS, ESQ.

Edited by
DEBORAH KEVIN

HIGHLANDER
PRESS

Smooth Sailing
Copyright © 2021 Cheri D. Andrews

ISBN: 978-1-7359333-1-3
Ebook ISBN: 978-1-7359333-2-0
Library of Congress Control Number: 2021935637

Published by Highlander Press
501 W. University Pkwy, Ste. B2
Baltimore, MD 21210

Cover design: Hanne Brøter
Cover photo: Sasha Khalabuzar (depositphotos.com)
Author's photo credit: Brenda Jankowski

In memory of my mother, Sandy, who brought me into this world, and my mom, Sue, who raised me, and together who modeled for me what it means to be a strong, resilient woman. You were my biggest cheerleaders. It was through your example that I was able, at fifty-nine-years-old, to completely reinvent myself and embark on a brand-new career journey. I hope that somewhere you are having a big old celebration in honor of your daughter becoming a published author. While I'm sure you would be proud of me, I KNOW that you are both shaking your heads wondering what took me so damn long!

LEGAL DISCLAIMER

Before you launch into this book, a Disclaimer.

1. This book is intended solely for educational purposes.
2. Nothing contained in this book constitutes or should be construed as legal advice.
3. Buying or reading this book does not create an attorney/client relationship between you and me.
4. If you have legal questions or concerns specific to your own situation, please consult with an attorney in your state.

CONTENTS

INTRODUCTION

You are the captain of your own ship; don't let anyone else take the wheel.
Michael Josephson

*A*s a small business owner, you are the captain of your ship. You come to your business with an entrepreneurial spirit and a willingness to roll up your sleeves, do the work, and get dirty. You are excited and enthusiastic. Being your own boss, setting your own schedule, working less (or, let's be honest, at least initially, a LOT more) hours, and being in charge of your own financial potential all hold a lot of appeal. But are you ready?

Before you launch your boat, you must go through a checklist to make sure that your boat is sound, you have enough gas to reach your destination, and you have all the provisions you need for a successful journey. Planning helps to ensure your journey is smooth. If you've already launched without completing the checklist, that's okay! You can still make course corrections for a safe journey.

IS THIS YOU?

As a small business owner, have you ever:

- Avoided consulting with an attorney because you find the whole process intimidating?
- Balked at the high hourly rates charged by law firms?
- Decided that legal do-it-yourself (DIY) is good enough for now?
- Wondered whether your business is legally compliant with regulations, but don't even know where to begin to find out?
- Operated under the assumption that the legal stuff can wait until later? Until your company is bigger?

Or ... maybe you haven't even given the legal aspects of your business a second thought?

> *Sticking your head in the sand might make you feel safer,*
> *but it's not going to protect you from the coming storm.*

— BARAK OBAMA

No matter WHAT your business is, LAWS are involved. And when it comes to the legal aspects of your business, ignorance is NOT bliss, because what you don't know CAN hurt you. In some cases, a simple course correction can bring you in compliance with laws and regulations applicable to your business. But in other cases, if laws are ignored or misapplied, they can sink your ship! Depending on how long you've been in business or the type of business you are involved in, much of this information may sound familiar. Or it may be completely new to you. There is no judgment here—just education!

You may think of the legal aspects of running a business as a necessary evil. I **challenge you** instead to consider the law as a tool to be leveraged for your success! I **challenge you** to consider your attorney as a trusted collaborator and ally, and one of your best resources for information on how to start, protect, and grow your business into a successful enterprise.

WHY DID I WRITE THIS BOOK?

I wrote this book because I love working collaboratively with small business owners to get the legal aspects of their business in order, so they can move forward with confidence that their livelihood is legally protected and legally compliant. Helping you make sure that all the good you are putting out in the world is protected really lights me up!

I wrote this book to help you avoid some of the most common legal mistakes that entrepreneurs make when starting and running their businesses, so you can make sure that your ship won't capsize because of a simple mistake!

I wrote this book to arm you with a basic understanding of the legal waters so you can ask the right questions when you consult your attorney.

I wrote this book to provide you with a broad overview of the most important things you need to be aware of when starting (or running if you are already there) your small business.

I wrote this book to educate you about what you don't know, what you can handle on your own, and when you need to call an attorney.

WHAT MAKES ME QUALIFIED ?

I have over thirty years of experience in both law firm practice and the corporate world as in-house general counsel for a small privately held company. I helped guide that company through a merger into a mid-sized regional company serving 95,000 subscribers and facilitating over 100 billion dollars in real estate transactions a year. But I'm not *just* an attorney. I'm also an entrepreneur just like you! In fact, I'm a multi-passionate serial entrepreneur.

My entrepreneur journey began at nine years old when my younger sister and I hosted our first "rummage sale" from the bedroom window of our ranch home in a suburb of Chicago, selling our toys to the neighborhood kids for a quarter each. My mom was, needless to say, not amused when she caught us! From there I graduated to babysitting, a paper route, and house cleaning, before getting my first W-2 job at the age of fifteen as an arts & crafts leader for a CETA (Comprehensive Employment and Training Act – a federal program in the 70's long since repealed) local summer day camp. For most of my legal career, I had a side hustle going—from making and selling crafts, to eight years of direct sales in the scrapbooking industry with a downline of over 100 women (while also running my own t-shirt design business), to owning a booth in an antiques and collectibles mall.

I've operated my businesses as both a sole proprietor and as a limited liability company (LLC). I understand what it means to start a small business. I understand some of the struggles you face. I understand how the vagaries of the market can dictate whether your business model succeeds or fails. I have been successful, and I have failed miserably. I have learned a lot along the way, and I've developed a real soft spot when it comes to helping solopreneurs and small business owners new to owning a business. The lessons I learned from my own experience, combined with my legal training, enable me to provide education and counsel to my clients to ensure that their businesses are built on a firm foundation and are legally protected.

WHO IS THIS BOOK FOR?

Whether you have a physical location with multiple employees creating or selling products or services, or you are a strictly virtual solopreneur selling goods or services to consumers or other businesses (or anything in between), this book is for you.

If you appreciate the value of good legal advice and are willing to pay an attorney to help you ensure your business is legally sound and compliant, this book is for you.

If you want to ensure that things are DONE RIGHT legally from the outset, this book is for you.

If you want to confer with your attorney armed with a basic understanding of the topics covered in this book, this book is for you. In fact, your legal fees will be less if your attorney isn't spending precious billable hours educating you!

This book is written based on United States law, (and sometimes specifically Pennsylvania law), but even business owners in other countries will find value in the general contract and policy concepts covered, which tend to be fairly universal.

Throughout this book, you will learn about legal requirements for small businesses. The discussion is intended to be inclusive of small business owners with less than twenty-five employees, entrepreneurs, solopreneurs, and creatives, terms which will be referred to inter-changeably throughout. Many of the examples are based on virtual service-based solopreneurs but the concepts are equally applicable to a company with twenty-five employees making and selling consumer goods from a physical plant.

WHO IS THIS BOOK NOT FOR?

The purpose behind this book is to educate you about the legal issues you may face in starting and running a small business so that you can make informed decisions that lead to better outcomes and to provide you with the basic language so that you will feel comfortable speaking to an attorney.

If you are looking for legal DIY or "how to," this book is not for you. To be perfectly clear, this book is NOT a legal DIY manual. Although we will discuss requirements to be compliant with various regulations, this book will not take the place of consultation with an attorney to draft your contracts and policies.

If you are expecting to find legal shortcuts or legal advice specific to your situation, this book is not for you.

If you anticipate your business will be publicly traded or need venture capital to get off the ground, you won't find advice on those specific topics here. Suffice it to say that securities law and financing are outside of my area of expertise. And I know to stay in my own lane!

If you have a brick-and-mortar location with employees, this book will not cover specific regulatory topics such as employment laws and Occupational Safety and Health Administration (OSHA) regulations. But you will find significant value in the more general aspects of starting and running your small business.

If you are a larger company that already enjoys an ongoing relationship with a business attorney, or maybe even has an attorney on staff (good for you!), this book may be too basic for your needs.

How to use this book

Read (or at least skim) the entire book. There is information in later chapters that will help inform decisions you need to make in earlier chapters. After you have a good understanding of the basics of launching a legally sound business, read through each chapter and create a checklist of things you need to do. Implement these steps one at a time. The order is critical to getting things DONE RIGHT and knowing that you are both legally compliant AND legally protected. To that end, you'll find a *Smooth Sailing* checklist at the back of the book. You can photocopy the checklist (or write in the book if you are a rebel) to use it as a guideline for ticking off steps as you complete them. Or you can download the checklist from my website at www. cheriandrews.com/checklist. Keep in mind that even if you have been in business for years, going through this checklist step-by-step to make sure everything was done properly can be very valuable. You'll catch potential mistakes, get them cleaned up, be investing in the longevity of your business, and be able to sleep better at night knowing that your business is legally DONE RIGHT.

If you are still with me, then it's likely that something in this Introduction struck a chord with you. And if that's the case, then you are itching to get to the good stuff ... so let's get started!

2

CHOOSING A BUSINESS ENTITY

*I learned this, at least, by my experiment: that if one advances confidently in the
direction of his dreams, and endeavors to live the life which he has imagined, he
will meet with a success unexpected in common hours. ... If you have built castles
in the air, your work need not be lost; that is where they should be. Now put the
foundations under them.*

Henry David Thoreau

$\mathcal{B}$uilding your business starts with moving in the direction
of your dreams, taking those first steps, whether bold or
tentative, to create what you have imagined. It requires a certain
passion for what you believe in to take those first steps, to take the
risk. Thoreau's words from *Walden* are inspirational and I have lived by
them since my teens. But it's the final statement that brings it home:
"Now put the foundations under them." If you intend to build a
viable, profitable business, you have to get practical fast.

The first key to launching a legally sound business is to choose a
business entity, the foundation for your business. What size boat are
you planning to captain: rowboat, luxury yacht, ocean liner?

In the business world, the business entity is your boat, the
container that holds your company. One of the most common

mistakes made by entrepreneurs is skipping this step entirely. So, their business has no structure, no firm foundation. For solopreneurs in particular, it may seem like an unnecessary complication. In some cases, it might be. But until you have discussed it with a professional, don't assume that you don't need a separate business entity.

There are two main reasons to set up a business entity: (1) to protect your personal assets and (2) to minimize your tax liability. Yes, under the right circumstances setting up a business entity can SAVE you money! A third, but seemingly less critical, reason to set up a business entity might be to lend additional credibility to your business. Being able to add "LLC" or "Ltd" or "Co" after your business name can provide a much-needed image boost.

What entity should you choose? The choice should align with your business goals and objectives. Is it going to be just you, or are you planning to scale up in the future? Do you eventually want to be publicly traded? Do you want to franchise? Will you have shareholders? Are you self-funding or will you need venture capital? Will you be selling your goods or services directly to the consumer or to other businesses? Your intended size and scope will help define the proper business entity for you.

This book will cover four primary legal entities that meet the needs of most small businesses. These are sole proprietorship, general partnership, corporation, and Limited Liability Company. We will talk about the features, advantages, and disadvantages of each entity type. There is no one-size-fits-all when determining which entity is the right one for your business. That decision should be made in consultation with your attorney and/or accountant in line with your personal business goals and objectives. I'm not going to delve too deeply into the C-Corporation or get into all the other options such as non-profit corporations, benefit corporations, and closed corporations as typically these vehicles aren't a good fit for a small business just starting out and looking to become profitable.

SOLE PROPRIETORSHIP

The sole proprietorship is the simplest entity. In fact, if you do nothing, it is the default. A business run by a single person that does not file any other paperwork with their state is automatically a sole proprietorship. The biggest advantage of the sole proprietorship is that it has the least upfront cost in terms of filing paperwork with the state. You may need some business permits or licenses in your local municipality or county. If you are selling goods or services subject to sales tax, you will need a sales tax license. But you don't need any incorporating paperwork, corporate resolutions or minutes, stock certificates, or other documentation of a corporation.

However, sole proprietorship, while tempting because there is minimal to no paperwork to file with your state, means YOU are the business. That is the biggest disadvantage of a sole proprietorship—there is no separate legal entity to protect you, so all of your personal assets, including your home, cars, and bank accounts are at stake in answering for the debts and obligations of, and lawsuits against, your business. You may be able to cover some of this liability through insurance with an appropriate general liability, professional liability, or business owner's policy, depending on your goods or services.

For taxation purposes, a sole proprietorship is considered a "disregarded entity" by the United States Internal Revenue Service (IRS). Your business profits or losses are reported on Schedule C of your personal income tax return and taxed at your individual rate. You are entitled to deduct the allowable costs and expenses of your business, but you won't be able to leverage all the tax deductions to which you might be entitled under another entity structure. You will pay income taxes on all of the net income of the business, including 15.3% (as of 2021) self-employment tax (Social Security and Medicare). This can eat significantly into the actual amount going into your pocket. A W-2 wage earner has half of that amount deducted from his pay, while the employer foots the bill for the other half. Additionally, Uncle Sam may be scrutinizing your return to determine if you are running a legitimate business and not just trying to claim tax deductions for a hobby.

The sole proprietorship works best for a single owner business who has a very low risk of liability for personal or financial injury to its customers or clients. For example, if you are a crafter making elegant greeting cards that you sell on Etsy or another online retailer, it is unlikely that your product would ever cause physical or financial harm to your customer. On the other hand, if you are selling those same greeting cards at a brick-and-mortar gift shop where you also sell beautifully scented bath products and candles, you have the potential for slip and fall injuries in your store or allergic reactions to your scented products. In this case, the sole proprietorship would not be the optimal entity choice for your business because of your increased risk of liability.

- **Primary advantages:** Easy to set up; low entry cost; no state filing other than fictitious name registration, if needed.
- **Tax Treatment:** IRS disregarded entity; profits pass through to owner's individual return reported on Schedule C.
- **Primary Disadvantages:** Owner pays 15.3% self-employment tax on 100% of profits; owner is personally liable for all debts and obligations of business.

FICTITIOUS NAME REGISTRATION

If you are operating under any name other than your proper legal name or the legal name of your business entity, you may be legally required to file a fictitious name (also "assumed name" or "doing business as") registration with your state. Check with your state corporation bureau for requirements. In some states, this can also mean advertising in both a legal newspaper and a newspaper of general circulation in your county, which can add to your startup costs. By way of example, in Pennsylvania anyone, whether individual or company, operating under a name other than their proper legal name is required to file a fictitious name registration. The current filing fee for a fictitious name registration in Pennsylvania is $70. Not bad. But if an individual (sole proprietor) is listed as the owner of the fictitious name, advertising is required under Pennsylvania state law. Advertising can run a few hundred dollars. Fictitious names where an LLC is listed as the owner do not need to advertise in Pennsylvania, however state law varies significantly.

PARTNERSHIPS

The partnership is the functional equivalent of the sole proprietorship when there is more than one owner for the business. For example, if you and your best friend decide to open a gym where you provide personal fitness coaching for your clients and small group classes, with a partnership, you will each have an ownership interest in the business. Absent an agreement to the contrary, you will both own 50% of the business.

Entering a partnership is like getting married. You will be spending a lot of time with your business partner. I highly advise you to enter into a partnership agreement at the outset, while your friendship and enthusiasm for your business are strong. The most common problem partnerships face is disagreements among the partners about who is doing more work, the direction of the business, what liabilities (loans, inventory, etc.) levels are acceptable, and the like. A well drafted partnership agreement works like a prenuptial agreement for your business marriage and will define your ownership percentages, your obligations to the business, and what happens in the event of death, disability, or divorce of one of the partners or a significant disagreement over the direction of the business, among other things. It should also cover what happens in the event you and your business partner decide to part ways.

Partnerships file an informational tax return, and the profits, losses, and expenses pass through to the partners in proportion to their ownership interest. Taxation on your share of the profits or losses follows the same general rules as the sole proprietorship.

- **Primary advantages:** Easy to set up; low entry cost; no state filing other than fictitious name registration, if needed.

- **Tax Treatment:** Information return for Partnership on IRS form 1065; Partners report their share of profits on Schedule E of individual return.
- **Primary Disadvantages:** Partner pays 15.3% self-employment tax on 100% of their share of profits; each partner is personally liable for all debts and obligation of business.

C-CORPORATIONS (C-CORPS)

C-Corps typically have shareholders, bylaws, a board of directors, and are required to maintain share certificates, regular meeting minutes, hold annual shareholder meetings, and file their own tax returns. C-Corps require a significant amount of paperwork and cost for filings with the state of incorporation up front, and then yearly filings and tax returns on behalf of the corporation. Additionally, if you are issuing shares, there are also state and federal securities laws to consider. But if eventually becoming publicly traded or selling your business is among your business goals, the corporate structure allows the business to grow, enjoy existence beyond the life of its incorporators, and make change of ownership easier. A C-Corp also allows for a public offering. The vast majority of publicly traded Fortune 500 companies and global companies are C-Corps. These companies are typically large with hundreds or thousands of employees and thousands or even millions of shareholders.

On the downside, C-Corps are subject to double taxation—first the corporation pays income taxes on its profits, and then the shareholders pay income taxes on the dividends they receive from those profits. Despite the issue of double taxation, C-Corps are the better option if you need investors or plan to grow significantly. Most venture capital backed start-ups are C-Corps.

The remainder of this book won't delve much into the C-Corporation structure as it is not one typically used by most small businesses or entrepreneurs.

- **Primary advantages:** Personal liability protection to shareholders; break on self-employment tax; fringe benefits are deductible as a business expense and not taxable to employees as income.
- **Tax Treatment:** Corporation files and pays its own taxes on IRS form 1120; Shareholders pay income tax on any dividends received.
- **Primary Disadvantages:** Double taxation; Much more expensive to set up; a lot more paperwork to maintain.

LIMITED LIABILITY COMPANY (LLC)

The LLC does exactly what the name implies—it provides *limited* liability protections for your personal assets by creating a separate entity that is liable for your business obligations, debts, and lawsuits. To be clear though, it won't provide protection against your own negligence, criminal acts, or tax obligations.

The LLC is a great option for self-funded businesses and can also work well if you are using a bank loan or borrowing cash from your friends and family as your initial source of business funding. The single member LLC is the simplest to form and is taxed the same as a sole proprietorship as a pass-through of profits or losses to the owner via Schedule C on IRS Form 1040. A multi-member LLC is taxed as a partnership with profits or losses passing through to each partner in proportion to their ownership interest.

An LLC has the ability to file fictitious name (or doing business as) designations as well, and in fact, may be required to do so in some states. Check the specifics of your state for requirements. Note that a fictitious name designation owned by the LLC retains the limited liability protections. However, if you file the fictitious name registration with yourself individually listed as the owner, you will lose the protections afforded by your LLC. This is another one of those little nuances where a simple mistake in the registration process can cause you big problems down the road!

The LLC also provides some great tax planning options by allowing you to be a sole-member or multi-member LLC but change the way your taxes are calculated. By making a Subchapter S or Subchapter C election, you can alter what items are allowable as business expenses, and how much you might be paying in self-employment taxes. This is where proper planning with your tax professional will permit you to maximize allowable deductions and minimize your tax liability. For these reasons, in my experience, the LLC is truly the best option for most businesses starting out (small shops, online services, professionals). The flexibility in structure facilitates your business growth and changes from solopreneur, to emerging business with a team of independent contractors, to a small business with employees and benefits!

ENTITY TYPE: SINGLE MEMBER LLC

- **Primary advantages:** Personal liability protection for owner.
- **Tax Treatment:** IRS disregarded entity; profits pass through to owner's individual return reported on Schedule C.
- **Primary Disadvantages:** Owner pays 15.3% self-employment tax on 100% of profits; some initial cost and paperwork to set up; possible annual registration fees.

ENTITY TYPE: MULTI-MEMBER LLC

- **Primary advantages:** Personal liability protection for members.
- **Tax Treatment:** Information return for LLC on IRS form 1065 or 1120; Members report their share of profits on Schedule E of individual return.
- **Primary Disadvantages:**Members pay 15.3% self-employment tax on 100% of their share of profits; some initial cost and paperwork to set up; possible annual registration fees.

SUBCHAPTER S-CORPORATION (S-CORP)

An S-Corp is not actually a business entity in and of itself. An S-Corp is formed by first filing as an LLC or C-Corp and then making a Subchapter S election by filing Form 2553 with the IRS. The Subchapter S election is a tax election that allows all income of the company to pass through to the owners. Instead of a Schedule C on your personal tax return, you'll be filing a Schedule E and you'll also be filing a tax return on behalf of the company and quarterly employer's federal tax returns. You will also be required to have annual meetings and maintain minutes ... even if, as a single member LLC with the S-Corp election, it means you are having the meeting with yourself! It is a significant additional amount of paperwork, so this needs to be weighed against the potential deductions to determine if the benefit is worth the work. Once a Subchapter S election is made, you will set up payroll (another cost to be considered) and employee benefits for yourself as the owner. You must pay yourself a reasonable salary, on which you will pay income taxes including the full 15.3% self-employment tax.

Expenses such as 401K or Simplified Employee Pension (SEP) IRA contributions, medical insurance premiums, and other benefits are allowed as business deductions, which lower the business net income. This structure allows you to receive the remaining net income (after salary and deductions) as a distribution and avoid the self-employment tax on that portion of business profits. But again, check the rules in your state. A few states tax S-Corps the same as C-Corps, and California charges a minimum $800 per year franchise tax on S-Corps. I know I've already said this, but it bears repeating —plan this out with your tax professional to determine whether or when a subchapter S election is right for you!

The downside of the S-Corp election is that S-Corps are not eligible for dividends-received deductions or the 10% of taxable income limitation for charitable contribution deductions. S-Corps may only be utilized for closely held corporations with a limitation of up to 100 shareholders, all of whom must be individuals (no company or trust can own shares). S-Corps work well for single member LLCs and family-owned or closely held companies that have no intention to grow beyond that 100-shareholder limit.

ENTITY TYPE: SINGLE MEMBER LLC WITH S ELECTION

- **Primary advantages:** Personal liability protection for owner; many tax advantages; only pay self-employment tax on income taken as salary, not on pass through profits; benefits allowed as deductions from income.
- **Tax Treatment:** LLC files information return on IRS 1120S; Member reports salary on 1040 and pass-through profits on Schedule E.
- **Primary Disadvantages:** Significantly more paperwork and tax reporting than simple LLC; must be at a certain profit level for tax advantages to outweigh self-employment tax.

ENTITY TYPE: MULTI-MEMBER LLC WITH S ELECTION

- **Primary advantages:** Personal liability protection for members; many tax advantages; only pay self-employment tax on income taken as salary, not on pass through profits; benefits allowed as deductions from income.
- **Tax Treatment:** LLC files information return on IRS 1120S; Members report salary on 1040 and pass-through profits on Schedule E.
- **Primary Disadvantages:** Significantly more paperwork and tax reporting than simple LLC; must be at a certain profit level for tax advantages to outweigh self-employment tax.

After discussions with several accountants and CPAs, there is a fairly wide range of opinion on the sweet spot for when you should consider making a Subchapter S election. As a tax minimization vehicle, the Subchapter S election is only an advantage when your business is actually profitable or if you are able to use losses to offset other personal income or the income of a spouse. Be careful with this, however, because losses may only be offset to the extent you are actually invested in the company. Many tax professionals advise that in the first year or two of business, if your numbers result in an overall loss or a break-even situation, you don't need the Subchapter S election. The potential tax savings are not worth the additional cost and paperwork. But once you become profitable? I've been advised as low as $10,000 net profit to as high as $50,000 net profit is required before the Subchapter S election really saves you money on taxes. How much you save is dependent on how much you pay yourself in salary versus how much you pass through. Keep in mind the requirement that you pay yourself a "reasonable" salary which will vary depending on your industry and the work you are doing. Discuss this with your tax advisor, making sure you understand both how conservative/aggressive your tax advisor's strategies are and your own risk tolerance.

Another consideration in business entity selection is the administrative costs. You'll want to compare total costs against potential benefits and tax savings. Costs to consider include:

- Initial filing fees and set up costs. These vary greatly from state to state.
- Annual costs for maintenance. Does your state require an annual report with a fee attached?
- Any state taxes on gross or net income.
- Additional costs for tax return preparation.
- Payroll expenses.

These costs will vary significantly based on the type of entity and the state in which you are filing.

From the discussion in this chapter, you can see that your choice of business entity truly does matter. Your choice of entity can impact many operational areas including:

- Taxes and filing requirements;
- Allowable business deductions;

- Legal obligations;
- Legal risks;
- How you approach your bookkeeping and accounting; and
- How you finance your business.

The choice should not be made lightly and consultation with professionals who can guide you in the right direction is highly recommended.

KEY TAKEAWAYS

- There are advantages and disadvantages to each type of business entity and there is no one-size-fits-all solution. The choice of business entity for YOUR business is highly individual and fact specific.
- For many solopreneurs and very small businesses, the LLC will be the most advantageous option for legal protection, growth opportunity, and tax advantages.
- Careful planning at the outset is critical because it dictates in many respects what you can and can't do in the future. Professional advice from an attorney or CPA is highly recommended before you determine which business entity is most appropriate for you.

3

CREATING YOUR LIMITED LIABILITY COMPANY

You must live in the present, launch yourself on every wave, find your eternity in each moment. Fools stand on their island of opportunities and look toward another land. There is no other land; there is no other life but this.
Henry David Thoreau

When you are ready to start your own business, creating a sole proprietorship is really as simple as filing a fictitious name registration with your state (if you are operating under anything other than your own name) and starting your work. A partnership is only slightly more complicated because, as previously noted, I strongly recommend that you create a partnership agreement at the outset. I'm not going to discuss incorporation (C-Corp) here simply because it isn't the most advantageous avenue for the vast majority of small businesses. The LLC is the preferred entity for most small businesses that need the liability protection, so let's talk a little bit about what is involved in setting one up. Hint: it isn't a single piece of paper filed with your state!

I'm going to focus on the single member LLC. A multi-member

LLC is much the same in terms of setup with the exception that you will have more than one member, you will apportion ownership in percentages among the members, and your Operating Agreement will need to discuss voting rights, exit strategy, and how to handle issues that may arise between members.

As we discussed previously, a single member LLC is a "disregarded entity" for purposes of taxation. So, the single member LLC does not file a separate tax return unless an S election is made.

The filing requirements and fees for an LLC will vary somewhat from state to state, so you will need to check with the Secretary of State's office or other bureau or department that handles incorporation in your state for the rules that apply to LLCs in your state.

An LLC can be "member managed" or "manager managed." In a single member LLC, it is typically member managed, meaning you, as the sole member, will manage the day-to-day operations of the LLC. In a manager managed LLC, either a member or a third party is appointed to handle the day-to-day operations.

BUSINESS PLAN

Don't do a single thing to set up your new business before creating a business plan. A great idea is one thing, but is it a needed product or service? How will you make money? Who is your target market? What is your competition? Once you have a brilliant idea, you want to do some research to flesh out whether that brilliant idea can be transformed into a viable business. Check out your potential competition—what are they charging? How are they delivering products and services? How will you differentiate yourself so that you don't become mere noise in the marketplace? The Small Business Administration (SBA) has great information on creating a business plan and what it should include, as well as sample templates to get you started. See the Resources chapter for a link to those templates.

FINANCING

Your LLC will most likely be funded by an initial capital contribution by you in exchange for your percentage interest in the LLC. With a multi-member LLC, each member will make a capital contribution and ownership interest will be proportionate to the amount of capital contribution, unless the members agree and specify otherwise in the Operating Agreement. The percentage of ownership also determines how profits and losses are allocated among the members. Another way you might finance your start-up expenses is by a loan—whether from family and friends or a bank. The loan should be noted as a loan in your Operating Agreement and, if you are borrowing from family or friends, you should have a clear agreement with the lender, documented in a promissory note, regarding the interest rate and loan repayment terms. To keep the IRS happy, you should pay a commercially reasonable interest rate. If the rate is too low or no interest rate is included, the IRS can "impute" an interest rate and require your lender to pay income taxes on the interest they *should* have earned. You really don't want to go there...so include a reasonable interest rate. It can be less than what a bank would charge but should be more than what your family/friend could earn by leaving the money in a savings account or government bond. Win, win for everyone!

MEMBER COMPENSATION

How do you pay yourself? Depending on how your LLC is taxed, you can pay yourself a regular salary, a share of the profits, or a combination of both. As a single member LLC taxed as a sole proprietorship, 100% of the profits are taxable to you as income and you will also pay self-employment taxes on the full amount. It doesn't matter if you take a regular draw from your LLC or you take the profits at the end of the year.

However, if you have made a subchapter S election, you'll want to apportion your earnings between salary and profits. You'll pay self-employment taxes on the portion allocated to salary, but not on the portion distributed as profits. Before you start thinking about skipping the salary and just taking *everything* as profit to avoid the self-employment tax, let me warn you that this kind of gamesmanship is a sure-fire way to bring the IRS knocking on your door and you don't want to mess with the IRS! You are **required** to pay yourself a "reasonable" salary based on your industry and the services performed before you can take advantage of the S election self-employment tax free profits. Also, always check for special rules for those in health, law, engineering, accounting, and architecture fields. For some reason, the IRS likes to treat these professions differently and impose stricter tax rules!

CHOOSING A NAME

Before you actually file for your LLC, you need to choose a name for your business. And before you settle on a name, you need to search your state corporation bureau records to determine if your intended name is available for filing in your state. If your intended name is available in your state, don't assume that means you are good to go. You also need to do a trademark clearance search to make sure you won't be infringing anyone's trademark! Refer to the Your Business Identity chapter for more detailed information about clearing your intended name. Note that the name of your LLC and the name you do business under do not necessarily have to be the same. You can have a business name such as Joe Smith Enterprises, LLC, but hold yourself out to the public as A-1 Accounting Firm. That's fine but check your state rules as you will likely need to file a fictitious name registration (also called "assumed name," "trading as," or "doing business as").

EMPLOYER IDENTIFICATION NUMBER (EIN)

The EIN is also known as a tax ID. Do you need an EIN for your small business? Particularly if you don't have any employees? If you are a sole proprietor or a single member LLC, it isn't absolutely necessary. You can do business using your personal social security number in place of the EIN. However, you may wish to have an EIN to avoid giving out your personal social security number. You may need an EIN in the event you wish to obtain a bank loan, business credit card, or business bank account. You will definitely need an EIN if you ever want to hire W-2 employees. Applying for an EIN is free, takes very little time, and can be usually be accomplished easily online. Given that it costs nothing but a few minutes of your time, why not go ahead and give your business its own number?

ARTICLES OF ORGANIZATION

Once you have the name issue settled and you are clear on what your business is going to do, you can file Articles of Organization (also known as "Certificate of Organization," "Articles of Formation," or "Certificate of Formation") in your state. Depending on the state, you may be able to do this completely online, or it may involve filling out paperwork and mailing it to the correct office. It will most certainly involve a filing fee and the amount varies widely from state to state. Most state websites provide either a fill in the blank style form or sample articles that you can use as a template to create your own. You can expect to provide the following information:

- Your business name.
- Your principal business address or where your business is physically located. If you are 100% online, this is likely your home address.
- Your registered agent office name and address; the name and address that you provide should be someone who is available **all** business hours to accept service of process on your behalf. Depending on your state, this could be you, a friend or family member, a member or employee of your LLC, your attorney, or anyone else willing to accept service on your behalf. My preference is to use a registered agent service for this so that you don't run into complications with service of process. It's an inexpensive way to ensure that you don't miss important legal papers and to keep your

own address (or that of family/friends) out of the public records.

- Your statement of purpose or why you are in business. What goods or services do you provide?
- Type of management. Are you member managed or manager managed?
- Duration. How long will your LLC be active? Go for the "perpetual" or "unlimited" option if available unless you are creating an LLC for a specific purpose with a limited (and known) duration.
- Signatures of the members of the LLC.

Be aware of any additional requirements specific to your state. For instance, in Pennsylvania you must file a docketing statement with your Articles of Organization. The docketing statement asks for additional information not found on the Articles of Organization form, such as your year-end date for tax filing purposes. Additionally, if you are a professional such as a doctor, lawyer, or accountant, make sure to check your state for any requirements specific to your profession. Some states require additional filings and fees for professionals while others don't allow professionals to form LLCs at all.

While we are on the topic, let's talk about online incorporation services. These services will, generally for a flat fee, file your registration with your state and, in some cases, send you a basic packet of incorporation documents. They give the false impression that it is as simple as a few mouse clicks and a document from the state. This simply isn't true! That document is just the beginning! And if the incorporation service doesn't take the time to truly understand your business model and objectives, it's quite likely that document won't be worth the paper it's written on.

My client Danielle was changing her entire business plan. She was leaving behind the work she had been doing to pursue a new venture and wanted to change both her business name and model. She hired an incorporation service to handle the paperwork, assuming they would properly handle getting her LLC changed over. When Danielle engaged me and I reviewed the paperwork, I found that rather than dissolving the old LLC and starting a new one, which would have been the cleanest option, the incorporation service had merely changed the name of her old LLC. They didn't even change the business purpose! So now Danielle had an LLC with a name change that still indicated she was conducting the old business. How frustrating for Danielle when she learned this! Danielle ended up paying double filing fees plus my time to have the LLC amended again to reflect her new business model, when it could and should have been accomplished under the original filing fee.

Danielle also had an Operating Agreement prepared by the incorporation service that was clearly a standard template—the only thing that had been changed was the cover sheet including her business name and address. A knowledgeable business attorney would have provided an Operating Agreement that was customized to Danielle's business and how she intended to operate. Cutting corners just isn't worth it!

I've run into similar issues with clients who filed their own LLC. Typically, the business purpose isn't correctly stated, or the type of management is misstated, among other issues. There is often a lack of awareness of the benefits of using a commercial registered agent service. Fully fifty percent of the LLC Articles of Organization I've reviewed on behalf of clients have had issues that required correction.

OPERATING AGREEMENT

Once your Articles of Organization have been approved by your state, you'll also want to put an Operating Agreement in place. For a multi-member LLC, the Operating Agreement works the same as a partnership agreement. It should set forth how the business will be run and the rights and responsibilities of each member, such as voting rights, ownership percentage, capital contributions, tax election, what happens in the event of death, disability, or divorce of a member, how to resolve disagreements over direction of the company, and dispute resolution. An Operating Agreement is also highly recommended even for single member LLCs and may be required by your bank for a business loan.

As mentioned above, an LLC is taxed as a sole proprietorship or partnership unless an S-Corp election is made with the IRS. How your LLC will initially be taxed should be included in your Operating Agreement. If you attempt to draft your own Operating Agreement, have it reviewed by a small business attorney before you sign to ensure that you haven't misstated anything or created any unintended legal, finance, or tax issues. Your small investment up front to get this document in order could save you a boat load of heartache and regret down the road.

Now you are ready to start business! Here are a few additional tips to keep in mind:

LICENSES AND PERMITS

Remember when I mentioned that my own entrepreneur journey began at the ripe old age of nine? On a warm spring day, bare toes snuggled into thick pink shag carpet, my sister and I opened the bedroom window as wide as it would go and set up our toy display on the window ledge. A pop-up shop decades before it became fashionable! In our small neighborhood word-of-mouth advertising spread quickly and it wasn't long before there was a line of children at our window, clutching loose change in their fists, eager to browse our selection. We even managed a few sales before we got busted! The authorities (Mom) stepped in and immediately closed us down for failure to obtain the necessary permits (permission) to operate a pop-up shop.

It is all too easy for entrepreneurs to jump into business as ill-informed of the requirements as those two little girls. But getting shut-down in the grown-up world isn't "cute" and comes with a lot more adverse consequences. Unfortunately, this is another area where state and local requirements vary so greatly that I can't provide much guidance in the confines of this book. You will need to do some detective work yourself to determine what licenses and permits you will need. If you are selling taxable goods or services, you'll need a state sales tax license, so that you can collect sales taxes and remit it to the state. You may need a professional license depending on what you do (beauty salon, barber, massage, CPA, architect, dentist, nurse, optometry, pharmacy, real estate, funeral director, physical and occupational therapy, are just *some* of the professions and businesses subject to licensing requirements), and you may need a permit to operate your business in your specific municipality. For help determining what licenses and permits you may need, try contacting your local small business association, chambers of commerce, municipality offices, and trade associations. Start with the SBA and look for agencies and offices in your area.

BANKING

Your LLC is a separate legal entity from you. It needs its own bank account! Different banks have different rules, but don't be surprised if your bank wants copies of your Articles of Organization, Operating Agreement, and your EIN.

You should deposit all income from your business into a bank account in your business name and pay all expenses for your business from that same account. DO NOT EVER commingle funds with your personal banking account. If you accidentally pay something out of your personal account that is a business expense, create an invoice to your business and reimburse yourself from the business account. Keep your books ship shape!

INSURANCE

Do you have a risk of liability? If you operate any kind of brick-and-mortar establishment where customers or clients are on your premises, the answer is definitely YES—four out of ten small businesses have a liability claim in a ten-year period and slip and fall is the most common claim. According to a SCORE webinar I attended, slip and fall settlements average about $35,000 while the cost of going to trial often exceeds $75,000. You want to insure against that risk! Even if you are 100% virtual, if your products or advice present any risk of bodily harm or financial injury, you'll want to consider general liability or professional liability insurance.

A business owner's policy may include liability coverage as well as property damage (think computers, inventory, etc.) and business interruption coverage. Talk with your insurance broker about what kind of coverage is right for you. See the Building Your Team chapter for a more extensive discussion on insurance.

CONTRACTS AND OTHER DOCUMENTS

Unless you have filed a fictitious name registration, use your full official business name (as filed in your Articles of Organization) on your contracts, stationery, business cards, website—anywhere that your name is presented to the public. This is important for maintaining that separate entity protection for your personal assets. Have checks made out to the business name, not to you personally. Sign all contracts and documents as an authorized signatory on behalf of the LLC. So instead of simply signing "Jane Smith," sign documents "Jane Smith, Owner, ABC Business LLC." This makes it clear that you are signing as an agent or employee of the LLC rather than as an individual, again maintaining the clear line of separation that protects your personal assets.

If you are using a fictitious name filed under your LLC, you will use your full business name followed by the name you are doing business under in the first instance of your name in a contract. It should look like this: "ABC Business LLC, d.b.a. Fun Business Name." After the first instance, you can just refer to "Fun Business Name."

ANNUAL REPORTS

Many states require LLC's to file an annual report and pay a filing fee to maintain your status as an LLC. Don't neglect this if it is required in your state! Failure to file the annual report may result in your LLC registration being revoked, which means you lose the personal liability protection and tax filing status of the LLC entity.

Clearly, creating your LLC involves much more than just filing a piece of paper with your state. As you can see from the discussion, there are many things to consider and decide before you even contemplate filing your Articles of Organization. Much of this work can be done yourself if you are willing to do your research, take your time with the applications (including reading all of the online help available from your state corporation bureau), and proceed with caution. However, if it all feels overwhelming, remember that help is only a phone call away. A small business attorney in your state can walk you through the entire process and ensure that it is all done correctly. Engaging an attorney may also save you time and aggravation in the business formation process, permitting you to spend your time actually working your business.

KEY TAKEAWAYS

- Take the time to create a business plan before you launch.
- Run a trademark clearance search on your proposed business name.
- Understand the legal and tax implications of your entity of choice.
- Get professional help in those areas that you find overwhelming or outside of your skill set.

4

BUILDING YOUR TEAM

Alone we can do so little; together we can do so much.
Helen Keller

*A*s a solopreneur, your success is limited by your capabilities and the finite amount of time you have to devote to your endeavors. When you supplement your skills and time with the skills and time of other professionals, with all hands on deck, you can accomplish more and do it faster. The second key to launching a legally sound business is don't go it alone! Many entrepreneurs make the mistake of believing they can (or have to) do EVERYTHING themselves.

As the captain of your ship, you need a CREW to help you on your journey. You may be a fantastic coach, but website design is not in your wheelhouse. Or maybe you are a diva at website design, but finances make you break out in a cold sweat. You know what you know. BUT—do you know what you don't know? Your crew is there to fill the gaps for the skills you don't have. Or the skills you simply don't have the time to handle. It may be more efficient to outsource some tasks and instead spend your time on income producing activity.

Unless you have the training or specialized knowledge there are four areas where you should definitely have a member on your team helping you:

- Legal;
- Insurance;
- Finances; and
- Taxes.

These are the professionals who will help LIFT your business above legal and regulatory compliance issues. You want solid relationships with a business attorney, a business insurance broker, a bookkeeper or accountant, and a CPA or tax attorney. In each of these areas, an innocent mistake could cost you your business and everything you have worked so hard to build. And you don't want the first time you call one of these professionals to be when you are already in trouble!

LEGAL

We all know the saying "an ounce of prevention is worth a pound of cure." Nowhere is that saying truer than in the legal arena. Seriously, the money you spend up front on an attorney to help set up your business entity or draft a contract for you may save you ten times as much or more down the road. It is often difficult to quantify the value of a solid contract or well-drafted policy because the goal is risk prevention, which beats litigation any day of the week! But you may never really know when a provision in your contract caused the other side to choose to settle rather than sue.

Attorneys can tell you horror stories about the messes they've cleaned up after the fact when well-meaning entrepreneurs chose to set up their business entity on their own and filled out the form wrong or entered a business deal with no contract at all or a poorly drafted

DIY contract and lost not only the value of the time they put in, but expenses and business goodwill as well when the deal went south. Many small business owners don't believe these things will happen to them ... until it does.

A BRIEF word about legal DIY. With the plethora of DIY legal websites and forms out there, you may feel comfortable appointing Mr. Google, Esquire, as your attorney. I know it's tempting. Please take my word for it when I tell you—DON'T! Using discount legal service providers that don't take the time to get to know you and understand YOUR business, or simply filling in blanks on prefab forms that don't address your specific needs, business goals and concerns, can leave you exposed to many problems that an experienced attorney can help you avoid. Get someone on your team who can provide peace of mind and ensure you are positioned for success! Ever heard the phrase *caveat emptor*? It means buyer beware. And with discount legal services and pre-fab forms, you generally get exactly what you pay for. End of public service announcement.

HIRING AN ATTORNEY

By the time you finish this book, you will have a list of action items to complete in order to ensure that your business is legally compliant and protected. Some items on that list will likely require the help of a small business attorney. For many entrepreneurs, the mere thought of hiring an attorney sounds worse than a visit to the dentist. Which is just one more in the myriad of reasons why you might not bother pursuing the legal aspects of your business. In fact, when I speak to groups, one of the most frequently asked questions is something along the lines of, "Hey Cheri, how would I go about finding the right attorney in my area?"

In all honesty, the process for hiring an attorney is very similar to choosing a physician. When searching for a new doctor, you ask friends, neighbors, and local co-workers for referrals. You search online and read any reviews you can find. And then you make a call.

If you are reading this book, you are looking for a business

attorney who specializes in representing small businesses and entrepreneurs. Or you may be looking for an intellectual property attorney
if you want to file for a trademark, service mark, copyright, or patent.
But not just *any* small business or intellectual property attorney. You
want someone who listens to your concerns and who you feel
comfortable talking to about what is going on with your business. You
want someone who "gets" you and your business. Ask your friends,
colleagues, and neighbors. If you can't find a fit there, call your local
bar association and ask for referrals. When you have names, Google
them. Look at the attorney's website, Facebook business page, and
LinkedIn profile. Do you like what you see? Does this attorney's
branding resonate with you? (In other words, is this a swipe right or a
swipe left candidate?) Does the attorney have favorable reviews and
testimonials from clients similar to you? Does the attorney provide
the specific services you are looking for?

Once you've narrowed down the list of names, it is time to make
calls to those who made the initial cut. Take advantage of those who
offer free initial consultations. And if you have strong contenders who
charge for the initial consultation, it may be worth investing in a
couple so you can find the "right" one. Because it is just as important
to have an attorney that you trust and have an ongoing relationship
with as a doctor you trust and feel comfortable with!

During that initial consultation, explore the following questions –
even before you get into the issues or concerns that have you making
the call!

- **Credentials.** Don't be afraid to ask, "Are you licensed to
  practice in my state (or in the state where I intend to do
  business)? How long have you been in practice? Have you
  handled other matters similar to mine? What made you
  decide to pursue this area of law? Has there been any
  disciplinary action against you?"
- **Cost.** Let's face it, as a small business owner you don't have
  the capital to throw at a problem the way the big companies
  do. You want an attorney that will pay attention to your

budget. But you also want to keep in mind that you often get what you pay for. Cut-rate firms are not as incentivized to spend the time to dig deep, really understand your business, and provide advice and documents specific to your business. Beware of the low-cost, rapid turn-around models that are plugging your name and state into a template with no consideration of state or industry specific requirements. With all of that in mind, ask your potential candidates, "How are your fees structured? Do you charge hourly and what is the rate? If hourly, will you provide a firm estimate of the cost to handle my matter? Do you offer flat fee or subscription options that fit my needs and will provide me with budgetary certainty?" When considering the cost of working collaboratively with a business attorney, keep in mind that this is an investment in the success of your business. What you pay up front for his or her services is a very small fraction of what it could cost you down the road if you get sued, have to rebrand, or end up in trouble with a regulatory agency.

- **Convenience.** Is it easy to make an appointment? Is the attorney willing to meet virtually? How far away is his office? How quickly did the attorney answer (or return) your call, email, or text message?

- **Caring.** Does the attorney appear engaged, personable, and genuinely interested in helping you resolve your concerns? Or is he distracted and rushing you through the consultation? Does she "get" your business and your objectives?

- **Comfort.** Arguably the most important consideration is your comfort level with the attorney you are speaking to. Are you okay sharing your personal/business information with this person? An attorney can't help you resolve your problems and concerns unless you can be completely honest with him or her about what is going on with you and your business.

What exactly can a business attorney do for you? Here's a list of a few of the services for which you might engage an attorney:

- Business Entity Formation. Helping you determine which entity is right for you, filing all of the required paperwork in your state, including getting a registered agent and an EIN. Monitoring and completing any ongoing filing requirements.
- Drafting contracts and policies specific to your business needs and objectives.
- Ensuring that you are legally compliant with any regulations that might be applicable to your small business.
- Updating and advising you on laws and regulations that may affect your regular business operations.
- Intellectual Property (IP). Pre-branding research and trademark clearance, filing for trademarks and copyrights, monitoring your IP rights, sending out Cease and Desist letters on your behalf.
- Litigation. From debt collection to IP infringement to defending you in the event of a claim against you arising from your products or services.
- Making referrals for other business resources such as tax accountants/attorneys, business insurance brokers, bookkeepers, etc.

Having an attorney on your team is integral to your long-term success. From the day-to-day operational issues, to reviewing the documents you are being asked to sign, from walking you through a purchase, sale, merger, or acquisition, to representing you in the event of a suit, your attorney is your legal lifeline. Don't leave sight of shore without one on board!

INSURANCE

Insurance is another tool for risk management. For a predictable fee (premium), you get to shift the risk for certain types of loss over to your insurance carrier. Just like auto or homeowner's insurance to protect your car, your home, and yourself from liability, you need insurance for your small business. The types of insurance you need to carry will depend on your business model, your industry, and the level of risk you are willing to self-insure. Types of insurance you will want to discuss with your insurance broker may include:

- **General Liability**. This covers the cost of your legal defense and damages for accidents or negligence. For instance, if someone slips and falls inside your retail store, or if your employee gets into a car accident while making a delivery for you and the other driver is injured. Note that General Liability coverage does not cover gross negligence or intentional actions on the part of you or your employees. For example, if your employee is driving while intoxicated, coverage will be excluded under the policy.

- **Professional Liability**. Covers legal defense and damages for claims arising from mistakes made by or improper advice provided by licensed professionals such as doctors and other health care professionals, lawyers, and accountants. This typically must be purchased separately from general liability coverage as it is specifically excluded under general liability policies.

- **Property Insurance** (similar to homeowners, renters, automobile, etc.). Covers the repair or replacement of property covered under the policy—it can cover damage to your office or store and your furniture, equipment, inventory, etc. for covered losses such as storm damage, fire, vandalism, etc. Be aware of the exclusions under the policy —some policies may require you purchase separate coverage for things like floods or hurricanes if that is a prevalent loss type in your area.

- **Product Liability**. This coverage is specific to the items you make and/or sell and covers you in the event a customer is injured because of a problem or defect in your product.

- **Business Interruption**. Covers your lost revenue for specific covered losses.
- **Business Owner's Policy**. This is a type of policy that often bundles liability, property, and business interruption into one convenient package and may be customized to fit your business.
- **Cybersecurity or Data Breach coverage**. Protects your business in the event your computers are hacked or sensitive customer or other confidential information is compromised. This is often a stand-alone policy but may be covered under some general liability or business owner's policies.

There are additional types of coverage available not included in this list. You should discuss your business model and insurance needs with a qualified insurance broker proficient in placing insurance for small business owners.

FINANCES

This section will be blessedly short because I am not a tax attorney and I don't have all the answers. But I do know some of the questions, which include:

- Do you need to collect and remit sales/VAT taxes?
- When should you file your business income tax returns?
- Are you required to make quarterly payments?
- What about payroll taxes like FICA, Social Security, Medicare, etc.?
- Does your business need to perform an audit of the books every year?
- Are you entitled to deduct medical premium payments, 401K contributions, mileage, education, meals, etc.? Are there limits?

Tax law is complicated (and often quite confusing), no matter the size, industry, or location of your business. If you don't happen have a degree in accounting, you may consider hiring a bookkeeper to maintain your business books and accounts regularly and a CPA or tax attorney to help you prepare your business tax returns. Bigger companies hire a CFO and staff to handle accounts receivable, accounts payable, payroll taxes, quarterly and yearly tax returns, audits, and all related documentation. Take your business seriously enough to get the help you need! Remember our earlier discussion about needing a team to help you navigate through the skills you don't personally possess? This is definitely one of those areas where you don't want to mess around!

If you have the business acumen, you can use accounting software such as QuickBooks to help you maintain your financial records. Start by implementing internal processes for accurate bookkeeping. If you've never maintained your own financial records and don't have the faintest idea where to begin, consult with a professional bookkeeper. They can help you get set up and teach you how to do the books yourself, or they can take this tedious chore off your to-do list, leaving you more time to do what you do best. Proper bookkeeping means you spend time each month working on your books—reconciling receipts, purchases, invoices—and making sure everything is properly categorized in preparation for filing of your year-end taxes. Staying on top of your books also provides valuable insight into your cash flow and profitability, allowing you to adjust pricing, expenditures, and volume to reach your financial goals for your business.

TAXES

Everybody has to pay them. Everybody hates them. Everybody NEEDS to understand them! Especially small business owners.

I've read that as a small business owner, you are three times more likely to be the subject of an IRS audit than a W-2 wage earner. If audited, you bear the burden of proving that your calculations are accurate. This is one reason why proper maintenance of your books is

critical. If you are sloppy with your bookkeeping and record maintenance, filing your taxes may be a nightmare. Defending an audit will
be even worse. Start by getting your books in order. Then talk to a tax
accountant or tax attorney about the best way to leverage your
numbers for maximum deductions and minimum taxes. We discussed
some of those tax considerations in the earlier chapter on Choosing a
Business Entity, but honestly only scratched the surface of potential
tax considerations and implications.

A well-qualified tax accountant or tax attorney will be able to guide
your business to legally and correctly maximizing income in your
pocket and minimizing taxes paid. Ask any entrepreneur who has
been overpaying self-employment taxes for years how much money
they were able to save once they began working with the right professional and you'll quickly see that working with a tax professional is
money well spent!

Another thing about taxes—the rules are constantly changing. As a
small business owner, it is a lot to expect yourself to keep up with all
the changes. That's where having a professional comes in handy.
Massive changes to the tax code were enacted in 2018, including
allowable deductions based on business type, and the rules on how
those deductions work. No doubt the tax code will be changed again.
But for now, we need to understand the tax benefits made available to
small businesses and how to implement and maximize them. The
single greatest expense in your entire life will probably be taxes. You
will, over the years, pay more in taxes than you will to get educated,
buy a house, or even raise children (although those are all expensive
undertakings)! For this reason, it is as important to learn how to
SAVE money as it is how to make money. Wouldn't you like to keep
some of that money in your own bank account instead of in Uncle
Sam's? A tax professional will know the up-to-date rules and regulations and may be aware of deductions you've never heard of! The
money you spend on a CPA is a deductible business expense and very
likely to save you more in taxes than you pay for his or her expertise.

EMPLOYEES V. INDEPENDENT CONTRACTORS

Beyond your LIFT professionals, at some point you may need additional help in other areas. Do you need an administrative assistant? A social media marketing specialist? A business coach? There are so many different kinds of help you could employ to grow and expand your business reach. Then the question becomes, are you ready for W-2 employees or should you hire independent contractors? What is the difference? What type of workers qualify as Independent Contractors?

Hiring a W-2 employee means you have control over when, where, and how they perform their work. You can require that they be present at your place of business, you can set the hours, and you have a lot of control over the tasks they perform and the order of performance. But having W-2 employees comes with a myriad of operational and regulatory requirements. You'll have to set up payroll and deduct appropriate federal, state, and local taxes from their pay and report and pay those taxes to the appropriate taxing authorities. You'll be required to cover half of the social security tax. You will also need to pay for workers compensation insurance and unemployment insurance.

If your employees are working from your place of business, there are OSHA regulations that must be met. Then there are the regulations on the human resources side of things—covering everything from job descriptions, employment applications, and interviews to hiring, onboarding, employee policies, Americans with Disability Act (ADA) compliance, discipline, and termination. Unless set up as a remote position, you will need to provide the space and all the materials and equipment necessary for your employee to do their job. Add to that the fact that most employers provide fringe benefits such as paid time off, holidays, medical and retirement benefits, and more and you will see that there is a LOT to consider when hiring your first employees and it won't be an inexpensive undertaking.

For these reasons, many small businesses start with independent contractors. If you find yourself needing general administrative help (answering the phones or emails, doing client intake, processing orders), bookkeeping services, social media coverage, or many other types of help, you can usually cover that need by hiring independent contractors. When you hire an independent contractor, you pay them an hourly or flat fee for defined work, but you do not deduct any federal, state, or local taxes or social security taxes. It is up to the independent contractor to pay those taxes directly on their own behalf. You do not have to provide workers compensation or unemployment insurance, paid time off, or any fringe benefits.

But you also give up control. An independent contractor decides when, where, and how they will accomplish the work they are contracted to perform. You may agree on hours spent on the work and deadlines, but ultimately it is up to the independent contractor. Generally, you are also not responsible for providing the space, equipment, or materials necessary for the independent contractor to perform their job. The independent contractor will provide their own computer, software, etc. Your responsibility is to complete a Form 1099-NEC at the end of the year and send it to both the IRS and the independent contractor for any person/company to whom you have paid $600 or more.

Your contract with an independent contractor can be set for specified projects or a specified length of time or can be open-ended with provisions for when and how either party may terminate the contract. Those provisions allow you to quickly break ties if you are unhappy with the work being done, without the headaches and paperwork involved in documenting and terminating a W-2 employee.

The one thing to be careful about is classification of workers. If you apply the independent contractor status to someone who actually operates as an employee, you can get into hot water with the IRS and may end up owing all of the taxes that should have been deducted from the fees paid to the worker. If you are in doubt as to whether a situation results in an employee or independent contractor classification, err or the side of caution and classify the worker as an employee, even if it is just for occasional part-time work. Alternatively, have the worker form an LLC, in which case, the worker is employed by his own company (not yours) and the IRS will likely accept this as proof that the independent contractor classification is correct. In this case, make sure that your contract is with the LLC, not the worker, and that checks for services are made payable to the LLC.

UNDERSTANDING WHAT YOU ARE CAPABLE OF HANDLING ON your own and when you need to hire experts or additional help is vital to the long-term health of your business. Making the right choices can keep your business successful and growing instead of leaving you dead in the water as you struggle to figure out things that are outside your area of expertise.

KEY TAKEAWAYS

- The four key areas to have a professional on your crew are legal, insurance, finances, and taxes.
- Hiring help in other areas outside your own skill set may allow you to spend more time doing what you do best – the work that produces your business income.
- Exercise caution when characterizing your help as employees or independent contractors.

5

CONTRACTS, CONTRACTS, CONTRACTS

A verbal contract isn't worth the paper it's written on.
Samuel Goldwyn

*A*t this point, you have your boat and your crew, but you still aren't quite ready to launch. You need to make sure you have the provisions for your trip. On a boat, that might be life vests, gasoline, food, and gear. In your business, from a legal perspective, it's your business contracts. So, let's talk about those.

The third key to launching a legally sound business is having solid contracts. Can you run your business without contracts? Well ... of course you can. And people have been doing it for literally thousands of years! So why am I making a big deal about contracts? This is another legal mistake made by entrepreneurs. Lack of a solid contract for the business you conduct can leave you exposed to legal risks that are easily avoidable. Using a solid contract, on the other hand, sets clear expectations between the parties and provides the opportunity to include legal protections that you don't get with a verbal or handshake agreement.

My client Amy is a perfect example of this. She is the founder of an executive level business coaching company. She entered into a collaboration with another coach, Linda, on the development of a group coaching program. Amy assumed that Linda's contribution was a work made for hire, while Linda assumed that they were entering into a partnership. Excited to work together, neither thought about documenting the relationship in a collaboration agreement in order to set expectations about their roles, their share in profits, or how they would handle disagreements. Amy had already developed the concept and most of the curriculum. Linda added value in coining a clever title for the program and enhancing the curriculum. As often happens in a collaboration, a dispute arose as to the value each brought to the table and the share of profits to which each was entitled. Amy wanted to part ways amicably, but Linda claimed intellectual property rights to portions of the curriculum, including the name of the program. In order to settle the matter, Amy was forced to rebrand her entire program at significant cost. She also suffered the loss of goodwill over the disagreement with Linda. All of which could have been avoided with a contract up front.

Before we dig into the type of contracts you might need and what should be included in them, let's do a little Contract 101 legal education.

What is a contract? A contract (also called an agreement) is a statement between two or more parties regarding an agreed upon exchange. A contract requires several things to be valid.

1. The first requirement for a valid contract is an *offer*. The offer must be specific in its terms. For example, you offer to create a website for your client for $5,000. You will likely go further and specify how many pages and elements the website will include for that $5,000.
2. The second requirement for a valid contract is an *acceptance*. Your client says, "Okay, I will pay you $5,000 to create my website." That is *acceptance*. But what if your client says, "I'd like to have you create my website, but I can only pay

$3,000?" In this case, there is no contract—this statement doesn't constitute an *acceptance*, it is a *counteroffer*. If you then agree and say, "I will create your website for $3,000" you have *accepted* your client's *counteroffer* and now there is a contract.

3. The third requirement for a valid contract is a *meeting of the minds*. This means that each party has the same understanding of the terms of the contract and that they all intend to be bound by those terms.

4. The fourth requirement for a valid contract is *consideration*. There must be an exchange of value between the parties. In most cases, this is goods or services being exchanged for money. But not always. Sometimes it can be a mutual exchange of goods or services or even rights, such as intellectual property rights. Without consideration, you don't have a contract.

5. The final requirement for a valid contract is *specific terms* such as the timing, the specifications of the deliverables or goods, and any conditions that must be met.

You might be surprised to learn that those legal protections I mentioned earlier are not actually required for a contract to be valid. In fact, if you purchase some of the contract templates available online, most of those legal protections will be missing. But those legal protections sure are nice to have in place and you'll be thanking your attorney for having your back when you are sued/need to sue to enforce a contract!

Contracts can be verbal or written. In my humble opinion, contracts should always be WRITTEN. Every. Single. Time. Because verbal contracts are simply too difficult to prove in court. A verbal contract gives rise to the classic "he said—she said" argument and unless you have some very strong witnesses who were there at the time the agreement was reached, you're basically left high and dry. So, get agreements in writing.

At this point, if you haven't nodded off on the sofa with drool running down your chin, congratulations! You've just survived day one of a law school contracts class. Thrilling, right?

Now that you know what a valid contract is, let's hit the basics of creating a contract. What are the fundamentals of a contract? I'm going to answer that classic reporter style – who, what, when, where, why, and how.

WHO. WHO ARE THE PARTIES TO THE CONTRACT? INCLUDE full legal names of the individuals or entities that are responsible under the terms of the contract. If you are contracting with another business, be sure the contract names the business as the party, not the individual with whom you have been negotiating.

WHAT. WHAT SHOULD THE CONTRACT INCLUDE? THE terms of the agreement you have reached should be formalized in a written document. A well-written contract should include all of the following:

- The obligations of each party;
- The rights of each party;
- The deliverables, what is being given (goods, services, or rights), and any requirements regarding quality, quantity, etc.;
- The time frame, or when each deliverable is due; or if it is an ongoing relationship, how long the contract will last and whether it renews or expires;
- The price along with any specific payments terms such as installments, late fees, interest, etc.;
- What happens in the event of a dispute; and
- All the legal protections. But we'll discuss those later.

WHEN. As I've already said, EVERY. SINGLE. TIME. No exceptions! No excuses! And the contract should be created as soon as the parties have reached agreement on the terms, before any work is done or goods or money change hands.

WHERE. With the advent of eSignature capabilities, the question of where is no longer a relevant issue. Executing (signing) a contract can easily happen without any of the parties leaving their home or office. And the advantage of eSignature is that (assuming you have a solid eSignature product) it maintains a log of exactly who signed when. It's awesome!

WHY. A contract is an excellent way to manage expectations. With all the terms of the agreement set out in writing, and an opportunity for each party to weigh in and clarify, everyone knows what is expected to happen and when, who is responsible, and what will happen if something goes awry. It's a way to allocate risk between the parties. It's a way to define dispute resolution procedures. It's a way to iron out all the kinks in a deal up front. It tells the story of how the relationship will play out at a time when the relationship is still in the shiny new stage and everyone is excited and agreeable.

HOW. Creating contracts should be a part of your everyday business process. You don't have to start from scratch every single time. Your attorney can create templated contracts for your routine work that allow you to simply change the name of the client or customer, the deliverables, dates, and price. Almost everything else can remain the same from contract to contract.

NEXT, LET'S DISCUSS THE TYPES OF CONTRACTS YOU MAY need.

SERVICE CONTRACTS

The first type of contract I recommend for most businesses is the service contract, which I also refer to as a client contract. This is the contract between you as the company and the client for whom you are providing products or services. A solid client contract spells out the price for your products or services, exactly when and what you are providing to the client for that price, any obligations on the part of the client that may affect your ability to deliver, and what happens if you or your client fail to meet your obligations under the contract.

Let's say, for example, that you are a coach located in Massachusetts. Your client is an entrepreneur located in California. Your coaching is all done virtually. Part of your coaching is assigning "homework." If your client routinely fails to do the homework, clearly, they won't get much out of the coaching arrangement. What happens then? Can the client demand a refund because they aren't happy with their progress? Are you obligated to continue moving the program forward when the client hasn't completed the foundational steps? If the client sues, will your matter go to court or arbitration? In what jurisdiction? A solid contract answers all these questions and more! It makes it a LOT easier to prevent a lawsuit or ensure that any lawsuit is brought in a forum that is convenient to you. Also, clear terms make a lawsuit less likely to ever happen in the first place.

VENDOR CONTRACTS

The second type of contract is vendor contracts. You undoubtedly have several vendor contracts in place that you don't even think of as contracts. For example, do use a website hosting company like Bluehost, GoDaddy, or SiteGround? No doubt you clicked through a Terms of Use for the domain name and the website hosting. That's a contract!

Are you using an email platform like HubSpot, Constant Contact, or Active Campaign? That's another contract. If you want to know all the companies you have contracts with, take a look at your accounting software and see which companies you are routinely paying subscription fees. And, QuickBooks, yep, another contract! Vendor contracts can also be with suppliers of the raw materials you need for production or the consumables used to run your business, with the companies that keep you stocked with office supplies, and with the companies that you pay for things like medical insurance premiums, liability insurance, payroll and accounting services, maintenance and repair of office equipment, etc.

You need to **be aware of the terms of these contracts** —especially whether the contract expires or auto-renews. If it auto renews—when? Is there a notice date for terminating? What are your options for ending the service? Can you cancel without penalty or are you locked into continuing fees?

This is an area where even large companies get tripped up. Software necessary to their infrastructure gets turned off because they forgot to renew, and they have to scramble to get a check out the door. Or they end up paying for an extra year for products/services they no longer need because they didn't give timely notice of their intention not to renew. Knowing your expiration/renewal dates is critical to managing your contracts.

TOOLS OF THE TRADE

While we are discussing vendor contracts, let's talk about a few of the tools of the trade you may be using. Admittedly, this topic isn't strictly a "legal" one, although I will briefly discuss the legal implications. But here's the deal … if you are taking your business seriously, you need the right tools for the job. And what those tools are will honestly vary greatly depending on your industry and business model. So keep that in mind as we go through this discussion.

ACCOUNTING TOOLS. I WANT TO START WITH THE MOST obvious, because this is something that EVERY small business owner has to consider. As we discussed in previous chapters, proper and diligent bookkeeping is critical to your success and to keeping the IRS happy. For the sole proprietor with a limited number of transactions, a good old-fashioned paper ledger may be a perfect tool for keeping track of your income and expenses. If you are a life coach who only handles ten clients a year in a high fee program or if you make and sell custom furniture and are only producing one piece a month, paper is probably sufficient and easy. But for the rest of us, I strongly recommend accounting software that links to your bank account and credit card processing. This keeps all that money stuff corralled. QuickBooks Online (QBO) is the most commonly used out there and has a variety of levels that should be sufficient to any small business needs.

There are competitors, but before signing up, please vet them thoroughly to determine if they have the features you need, provide the customer support level you expect, and allow you to transport your data if you decide to switch providers. READ (I know it is very rare that a small business owner does this) their contract and Terms of Service so that you know how they are using and securing your client's data. As I'll discuss later, the regulations under GDPR provide that you can be jointly liable with your service providers for the misuse or breach of client data!

Having chosen your accounting software, set up internal processes for ensuring that all of your expenses and income are captured in the software. This will make tax time so much easier!

 Pro Tip: Take my word for it … if you have categories set up that match the line items on your Schedule C (or other tax filing documents) it will be simple to transfer the totals! You'll thank me for this tip—your accountant will thank you!

PAYMENT PROCESSING. VERY FEW BUSINESSES THESE DAYS operate on a strictly cash or check basis. It's inconvenient for your clients and it often takes longer to get paid. So you may find yourself needing a payment processing service so that you can accept credit cards. Here again, the options can be overwhelming! QuickBooks and PayPal both have payment processing options for small businesses. If you already have a PayPal account, setting up with them is super quick and easy. Ditto with QuickBooks. If you need to be able to accept payments at point of service (in person) as opposed strictly online, you can look at options such as Stripe or Square. I'm not providing links or recommendations, because there are so many options and I haven't personally checked them all out. But I have clients successfully using each of these options. You might also have options directly with your banking institution. Compare your options, including fees, ability to integrate with your other tools, and convenience. It's easy to research via Google or your favorite web browser. Again, I advise you to READ the Terms of Service to understand how your client info is being used, how long it is being retained, and when/how you are able to terminate the services.

APPOINTMENT SCHEDULING. IF YOUR BUSINESS REQUIRES that you have appointments to meet with clients either one-on-one or in class settings, a good appointment tool can save you tons of time and money. As an attorney, I meet with clients one-on-one. So, I can either have them call or email me to schedule an appointment, which interrupts the flow of whatever I'm working on or, if I'm busy, they have to leave a message and then those stack up and result in tele-phone tag or a series of email messages back and forth to choose a time. I could hire a virtual assistant to handle scheduling, but then I'm paying for someone's time just to schedule appointments. I'm trying to keep my overhead low, so a scheduling app works perfectly for me!

Some of the more common ones include Calendly, Acuity Sched-uling, Square Appointments, Setmore, and HoneyBook. They all have different features and price points, so a little research to choose one is in order. I started off with Calendly but was only a month or two in when I discovered some limitations in their program that created issues for me. I switched to Acuity Scheduling which has worked out perfectly for me. No more emails back and forth to schedule client calls. I just email my client a link to my Acuity scheduler. They can see all of my available times and choose the one that best fits their schedule! If they need to change their appointment, they can do that via a link in the confirmation email. I've integrated Acuity with my Zoom account, so my calls are scheduled as Zoom conferences which allows me to see my clients, and to share my screen to review contracts and documents.

You can also use an app specific to your industry. For example, my massage therapist uses an online tool called massagebook.com. My gym uses WiX. WiX is fairly well known for developing websites, but they offer many additional tools and, in the case of my gym, they use the tool designed for purchasing packages and memberships and booking class sessions.

CUSTOMER RELATIONSHIP MANAGEMENT (CRM). ANOTHER tool to consider investing in is a good customer relationship management tool. The big companies use Salesforce, and other similar tools. The Salesforce price point isn't geared to small business. You can look at tools such as HubSpot, PipeDrive, Vtiger, Zoho, FreshSales, and others. Your goal here will be to find a platform that is simple to learn the ropes, affordably priced, provides good customer support, and has the ability to scale as your business grows. Bonus points if it works with your social media platforms!

The point is, whether you use an excel spreadsheet to track your customers, rely on your email marketing platform, or have found the perfect app, you need a way to keep track of your clients, customers, prospects, referral partners, and vendors. As a small business, you can always start with an excel spreadsheet and transition to a CRM tool when you can afford it.

EMAIL MARKETING. WE'VE ALL BEEN TOLD, REPEATEDLY, that marketing is the only way to bring in clients/customers. Marketing takes many forms:

- Print advertising: brochures, flyers, post cards, business cards, billboards;
- Social media posts: Facebook, Instagram, Twitter, LinkedIn, YouTube, TikTok, and many others;
- In person 1:1 meetings, called coffee chats, connection calls, discovery calls, and more;
- Group networking meetings;
- Speaking gigs; and
- Classes, workshops, and webinars.

Yet, the single biggest return on investment, according to every marketing expert I've talked to, heard speak, or watched a webinar from, comes from good old-fashioned email marketing!

I'm not going to spend a lot of time on email platforms. I'm not that familiar with the feature sets and cost of the various platforms. Just know that if you are going to have an email marketing list, you are going to need a service and you want to make sure it is CAN-SPAM compliant.

For the email marketing virgins, or those with a very limited budget, MailChimp is free for up to 2,000 contacts. The service is compliant with all federal CAN-SPAM Act regulations, which provides a lot of peace of mind. MailChimp has a simple, easy interface and tutorial videos so it's perfect for email marketing newbies. It also integrates with several platforms for additional ease of use. Additional platforms that offer free plans to get you started include: AWeber, MooSend, MailerLite, Zoho Campaigns, and Send In Blue.

Constant Contact is among the largest email platforms and also among those that have been around the longest. Although they don't have a free product offering, Constant Contact's focus is on email marketing newbies and small businesses. The interface isn't as slick as some of the competition, but it has added a number of tools including hundreds of pre-made design templates, contact management, and reporting.

Additional platforms you might consider include HubSpot, Active Campaign, and ConvertKit. And that's just the beginning. Google email marketing platforms and you'll get 314 million results. You can compare products and features, read reviews, and test drive the platforms that interest you.

DEPENDING ON YOUR INDUSTRY, THERE ARE LIKELY MANY additional tools you'll find useful to your daily tasks. Anything that can be automated and save you time, that you can then spend on income generating activities, is worth looking into. One other thing to consider as you begin cobbling together your toolset is whether the tools have integration capability. It's great if your payment processor and your bank have the ability to integrate with your accounting software so that income is automatically recorded, rather than you having to add it manually.

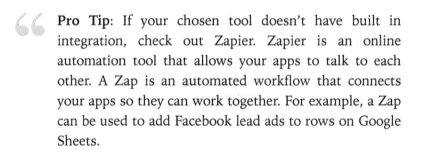

Pro Tip: If your chosen tool doesn't have built in integration, check out Zapier. Zapier is an online automation tool that allows your apps to talk to each other. A Zap is an automated workflow that connects your apps so they can work together. For example, a Zap can be used to add Facebook lead ads to rows on Google Sheets.

RECALL THAT ALL OF THESE TOOLS OF THE TRADE ARE vendor contracts, and you should maintain some method of monitoring your contracts for payments, renewal or termination dates, and notification requirements. I offer my clients contract management services where I track all of this for them and notify them when they need to take action. You might set up an excel spreadsheet and calendar notifications to accomplish the same thing.

NON-DISCLOSURE OR CONFIDENTIALITY AGREEMENTS (NDA)

NDAs are crucial if you are sharing your ideas, business plans, inventions, or processes with others for any reason. You want to make sure that they can't steal your confidential information and use it for their own gain. Use a one-way (unilateral) NDA when you are sharing valuable information in settings such as a pitch meeting or negotiations with a new potential client. Use a mutual NDA if both parties to the agreement are sharing information, such as in a collaboration or joint venture.

INDEPENDENT CONTRACTOR AGREEMENTS

If you are working with independent contractors (such as a virtual assistant or web designer), you'll want an agreement on the price and scope of their services. If they are creating content or design for you, the agreement should include a representation that it is their original work, indemnification against IP infringement, and a specific assignment of the IP rights to the final product or a clear license for your use of the IP.

LEASE AGREEMENTS

Unless you are a completely virtual business operating out of your home (or wherever your nomadic existence has taken you at the moment), at some point you will need to consider your space. Whether you need a store front building for your boutique clothing shop, an office where you can meet with your coaching clients, or a warehouse where you assemble, store, and ship your custom candles, your space needs raise a lot of questions. Should you rent, lease, or buy? Obviously, the answer is a resounding, "It depends." It depends on your business model, industry, rate of growth, long term plans, etc.

If you need space outside your home, the simplest option is to rent under a "full-service" lease agreement. The full-service lease agreement, similar to renting a home or apartment to live in, means you are purchasing space at a set monthly rate for a fixed period of time. The monthly lease fee includes not just the space, but also property & general liability insurance, taxes, maintenance, utilities, trash removal, etc. Your total costs are very clear up front. For the most part, people are familiar enough with a standard apartment rental contract that this looks familiar and they don't get too worked up over it.

A "net" commercial lease, on the other hand, can be downright petrifying. If you haven't encountered this type of lease before and you are handed a forty-or-fifty-page document to sign, you might be taken aback. My client, Chris, experienced this overwhelm when faced with a fifty-page lease agreement for a small commercial store front. She wisely reached out to me for a consult.

Under a "net" or "hybrid" commercial lease, your monthly lease payment is only a portion of your ultimate cost. You may be charged separately for metered usage on utilities, costs of trash removal, maintenance of your space, cleaning, and a share of the liability insurance and property taxes based on your percentage of space to the whole of the building. You may also be contributing to maintenance and costs for any "common" space such as lobbies, elevators, exterior windows, landscaping, etc. Some leases for commercial retail space even require that you pay a percentage of your sales to the landlord. Before signing off on one of these lease agreements, make sure it has been fully reviewed and that you understand all of the provisions. An escalation clause may allow your lease payment to be raised a specified amount every year. A use clause may limit what you can and can't do in the space or what you can and can't sell. It is important that you know what these provisions mean so that you aren't caught in the position of inadvertently breaching your lease agreement.

After a thorough review and consultation, my client Chris was able to negotiate changes to her lease agreement to limit her potential liability, cap rate increases, and clarify obligations regarding common space and things like plumbing and electricity. The lease as worded would have obligated to her to treat the space as if she owned it, being responsible for everything that might need repair or replacement.

Being able to clearly transfer some of that burden back to the property owner provided Chris with peace of mind.

This list of contract types is by no means exhaustive, but it should at least get you started in thinking about your contractual needs.

LEGAL PROTECTIONS

As mentioned earlier, contracts are a good place to set out necessary legal protections for your company. A good contract includes both business terms (the essence of the agreement between the parties) and legal terms (the protective measures in the event there is ever a dispute between the parties). Your legal terms will include things such as what state law governs, where a lawsuit can be brought, limitations on liability, who pays what in the event of a suit, and so much more. In this next section, we'll talk about some of the basic legal protections or terms that you may wish to incorporate in your business contracts.

CHOICE OF LAW. THIS PROVISION DEFINES WHAT STATE law will govern in the event of a dispute. Generally, as a business owner, you will choose the law of the state where your business is located, unless you have a specific reason to choose otherwise. But this does happen! For example, California law leans heavily to protection of the consumer. If your business is located in California, you may choose to apply the law of a jurisdiction that is more business friendly.

 Pro Tip: What happens if the parties to the contract are in different states? Each party is likely to want their own state law to apply. If you can't agree, a compromise position that has worked well for me in the past is to use Delaware as your choice of law. Delaware has a rich history of contract law that tends to be even-handed in dealing with contractual disputes.

JURISDICTION AND VENUE. JURISDICTION AND VENUE determine WHERE any lawsuit will be brought. Jurisdiction defines the state and court system in which a legal claim may be filed. Venue typically defines the county in which a claim may be filed. Again, as a business owner, you will want jurisdiction to be in the state in which you are doing business and will most likely specify venue in your own county. If your business is a business to consumer model it is usually straightforward to include this provision. However, if you are a business-to-business model crossing state lines, it may not be so simple. The other party may want jurisdiction and venue in their home state. Then you are faced with trying to understand which of the two states has the most significant "contacts" with the contractual matter, what legal and financial risks are involved in potentially litigating in another state, and how badly you want this business deal to move forward.

Sometimes the other side needs your goods or services badly enough to agree to jurisdiction and venue in your state. Other times it may be that you need the sale enough to agree to jurisdiction and venue in their state. I've used a few compromise solutions in the past as well. One is to choose a neutral state, such as Delaware, for any litigation. This means both parties will have to retain counsel outside of their own state which often encourages compromise and acts as a good deterrent to filing suit. The other tactic, and an even stronger deterrent to filing suit, is to specify that either party must bring suit in the other party's state. In essence, using this provision provides the defendant in the lawsuit with home court advantage and operates as a means of encouraging informal settlement of grievances. I have never had a lawsuit filed where this provision was included in the contract. Despite that, it still isn't my go-to provision. It is reserved for those instances where the other party simply will not agree to jurisdiction and venue in my client's home court.

DISPUTE RESOLUTION. DISPUTE RESOLUTION ALLOWS YOU to choose methods of resolving disputes short of actual litigation in court. Dispute resolution provisions may include:

- **Informal resolution**. The parties talk out their differences and reach a compromise that can be memorialized in an agreement.
- **Mediation**. The parties engage a neutral third party, known as a mediator, who meets both jointly with the parties and individually in an effort to understand the nature of the dispute and determine if a consensus can be reached on resolving the dispute. Mediation is not binding and if the parties cannot reach an agreed resolution to their differences, the matter may proceed to litigation.
- **Arbitration**. Arbitration operates like a mini trial with either a single mutually chosen arbitrator or a panel of three arbitrators with each side choosing one arbitrator and the two arbitrators selecting a neutral third. The matter proceeds in front of the arbitrators much as a trial would but with more relaxed evidentiary rules. After both parties have presented their case, the arbitrators confer and render a judgment. Arbitration is typically binding but may be appealed to the county/state court.

REPRESENTATIONS AND WARRANTIES. THIS IS YOUR opportunity to set forth the basic premises upon which you are relying in entering the Agreement. A representation is a statement of fact on which the parties are relying. Typical representations may include:

- The party is authorized to enter the agreement;
- None of the obligations the party is entering into under the agreement conflict with obligations to a third party; and
- Assertions regarding specific licenses, permits and approval.

A warranty is a promise that a condition or fact is true, with the implication that the party will provide indemnification if the condition or fact is false. Typical warranties may include:

- The party will comply with all applicable federal, state, and local laws and regulations in carrying out their obligations;
- Goods or services will meet defined quality standards, including that the labor and materials may be covered for defects for a specified period of time;
- Services will be completed in a professional and workmanlike manner; and
- Assertions regarding intellectual property rights.

The breach of representations and warranties are generally considered material to the contract and give rise to rights and remedies specified in the contract.

INDEMNIFICATION. INDEMNIFICATION CREATES AN obligation on the part of one party to pay defined costs and expenses on behalf of the other party for breach of the representations and warranties or other material provisions of the contract. This clause is critical in any contract for software or where the party you are contracting with is doing any kind of work for you that is subject to intellectual property rights.

NON-COMPETE AND NON-SOLICITATION. A NON-COMPETE clause prohibits one party from entering into business relationships or creating a business, product, or service that would complete with the other party. A non-solicitation clause prohibits one party from soliciting the employees or customers of the other party to enter into either an employment or customer relationship with the soliciting party. Both of these clauses are designed to protect the business dealings of the party which the clause favors. However, these clauses can be difficult to enforce. Courts, if they will enforce them at all, want to see reasonable limitations on the length of time and the geographical area that the clause is intended to cover.

DISCLAIMER. A DISCLAIMER IS A STATEMENT DENYING responsibility or liability for specific acts or omissions. The disclaimer's purpose is to prevent or mitigate potential liability. Disclaimers tend to go hand-in-hand with limitations of liability.

LIMITATION OF LIABILITY. LIMITATIONS OF LIABILITY restrict the amount and types of damages for which a party may be liable under the contract. As not all types of damages can be covered by insurance, it is important to limit the types of claims and to cap the amount that can be recovered in instances of personal injury or financial loss. A frequent strategy is to cap damages at the amount received in payment for the goods or services being sold.

In order to be enforceable, both the disclaimer and limitation of liability clauses should be written to clearly and unambiguously express the intentions of the parties and appear conspicuously within the agreement. The "conspicuous" requirement is why you generally see these two clauses appear in all capitals within a contract document. Case law has dictated that these clauses be called out to the attention of the signatories and the all caps is an approved method of doing so.

TERM AND TERMINATION. TERM AND TERMINATION COVERS how long the contract is intended to last, the reasons for which a party may terminate the agreement, any notice required for termination, and what happens once an agreement is terminated. Term can be stated as a specific length of time or can be perpetual until either party takes action to terminate the agreement.

Many vendor contracts are set up as a fixed term, meaning monthly or yearly terms that automatically renew for another term unless a party has given notice of their intention to terminate. In some cases, the agreement is for a fixed term and then terminates automatically. If goods or services are still needed after the termination date, the parties will execute a new contract. Both my legal research software and my professional liability insurance are set up this way.

Sometimes with contracts like this, you can negotiate an extended term in exchange for guaranteed pricing or a percentage cap on yearly increases. This provides the seller with guaranteed revenue for a period of years and provides the buyer with predictability in their budget. In all fixed term agreements, the contract will either automatically renew or terminate at the end of the term. With automatic renewal contracts, there is usually a notification period during which a party can provide notice of their intent not to renew, allowing either party to end the agreement before the next renewal term.

The termination clause defines what happens when the agreement comes to an end. If the agreement is not terminated by a fixed term, termination may occur for cause (one party is not living up to expectations under the agreement) or for convenience (either party decides they do not wish to continue the relationship through no fault of the other party). Termination may require final payment of all work completed to the date of termination, return of confidential materials, and other specific actions to finalize the agreement.

ASSIGNMENT. ASSIGNMENT DEFINES WHETHER OR NOT A party can transfer their rights and obligations under the agreement to another party. If you don't specifically state in an agreement that assignment is not permitted, the presumption will be that it is allowed, with the exception of intellectual property rights which require specific consent to transfer. You may wish to allow assignment in the event your company is ever sold, merged, or acquired so that you don't have to redo all of your contracts. You may wish to prevent assignment in cases where you have hired someone for their unique talent and skills and don't want them to pass off fulfillment of the contract obligations to another party.

FORCE MAJEURE. THIS CLAUSE TYPICALLY EXCUSES THE parties from performing their obligations under the contract if causes outside of their control prevent them from doing so. Causes can include everything from war, riots, and pandemics to natural disasters such as floods, hurricanes, and earthquakes that may cause power outages and property damage. This clause can specifically enumerate *force majeure* events or can leave that open to interpretation of the parties and courts.

SEVERABILITY. A SEVERABILITY CLAUSE IN A CONTRACT states that the contract terms are independent of one another so that if one or more provisions are declared unenforceable, the rest of the contract will remain in force. Basically, this provision allows a court, after voiding one or more terms of the contract, to interpret the remainder of the contract to (as nearly as possible) effectuate the intent of the parties. Sometimes, severability clauses will state that certain terms of the contract are so integral to the purpose of the contract that should those provisions be determined to be illegal or unenforceable, the contract as a whole fails of its essential purpose and cannot be enforced.

ENTIRE AGREEMENT. THE LANGUAGE "ENTIRE AGREEMENT," also known as an integration clause, is used to prohibit a party from relying on oral statements, emails, letters, or other documents outside of the agreement to establish the terms of the agreement. Basically, whatever is expressly set out in the agreement is the entire agreement and the parties are not relying on anything else in entering the contract.

THERE ARE ADDITIONAL LEGAL PROTECTIONS YOUR attorney may add such as waivers, confidentiality, releases, and more. Which legal protections are included will depend on the type of the contract and the relative risk situation. Your contract should be customized to address the type of business you are conducting and the risk allocation between the parties of the potential risks of the agreement.

When your agreement is drafted and ready for execution, pay attention to how you sign! A sole proprietor can sign their own name because, as we discussed in the Choosing a Business Entity chapter, as a sole proprietor, you are the business. There is no separate entity.

If you are using a fictitious name (also known as a DBA or "doing business as"), you'll want to have that fictitious name above or below your signature block. But if you are signing a contract as a member of an LLC or a shareholder of a corporation, you want to make sure you are signing on behalf of the business, and not as an individual. In this case the signature block should have the name of your company above the signature line, then BY: in front of the signature line, and your name and title below the signature line. Like this:

ABC Company, LLC
By:_____
Amy B. Smith, Member

The title can be member, manager, or any other title you use for your position in the company such as owner, president, CEO, Divine Goddess, etc.

Once you have contracts that you are routinely using in your business, keep in mind that laws are changing all the time. Your contracts should be reviewed and updated yearly to account for any changes that affect your terms. For example, at the time of writing this book, many business owners were scrambling to update their *force majeure* clauses to ensure that pandemics are covered.

KEY TAKEAWAYS

- Contracts provide the opportunity to set expectations, determine how disputes will be resolved, and provide for legal protections to mitigate risk.
- Contracts should be a part of your everyday business practices.
- Make sure you sign contracts on behalf of your business, not as an individual.
- READ the terms of service for your vendor contracts.
- Know the terms of your contracts, particularly termination and notice requirements.

6

POLICIES AND PROCEDURES FOR COMPLIANCE

You have to learn the rules of the game.
And then you have to play better than anyone else.
Albert Einstein

*W*ere you aware that boating on navigable waterways in the United States is regulated? That your activities are restricted in order to protect certain vulnerable areas? This is something your boating buddies will share with and explain to you as you begin your own boating venture. Or you'll find out about the hard way when your boat gets pulled over by the Coast Guard because you are somewhere you shouldn't be or doing something you shouldn't be doing!

We know you are a smart captain and you've done your homework. When your boat finally leaves the dock, you'll have the peace of mind of knowing that you've filed a float plan with your local marina and a few trusted friends and you're cognizant of all the marine and fishing regulations designed to protect the vulnerable waterways you plan to travel. After all, you want to be sure you aren't doing anything to draw the negative attention of the Coast Guard, and conversely, that they know where to find you in the event of trouble.

In your business there are also laws and regulations with which you must be compliant. But who is sharing this information with you? And where do you turn to find out on your own if you don't have an appropriate mentor to clue you in?

The fourth key to launching a legally sound business is establishing policies and procedures for compliance. Your policies and procedures are critical to ensuring that your business is protected from regulatory nightmares. Almost all of the policies and procedures you will establish for your business are driven by the need to comply with specific statutes, rules, and regulations. While it may feel like overkill to think that your solopreneur consulting business needs policies and procedures, it's actually quite important! Thinking you are too small to need policies and procedures is another legal mistake unwittingly made by unwary small business owners. As former U.S. Deputy Attorney General Paul McNulty said: *"If you think compliance is expensive, try non-compliance."*

There are a number of policies and procedures you might consider implementing. What we can touch upon within the confines of this book will only scratch the surface. What follows is by no means exhaustive but covers some of the most common policies you should think about.

WEBSITE POLICIES

Website policies refers to those policies that cover information available on your website and information collected via your website. From the familiar privacy policy and terms of use to the less familiar disclaimers and copyright provisions, this section will cover a number of website policies you may wish to incorporate into your website and your business operations.

WEBSITE PRIVACY POLICY. DOES MY WEBSITE NEED A privacy policy? I get asked this question all the time! The answer is almost always a resounding YES!

- If you have a newsletter sign up form on your website with which you collect names and email addresses, you need a privacy policy.
- If you have a free offer or lead magnet that you use to collect names and email addresses, you need a privacy policy.
- If you have a contact form or scheduling link with which you obtain names, emails, or phone numbers, you need a privacy policy.
- If you use cookies that collect IP addresses and consumer behavior, you need a privacy policy!

Basically, unless your website is a static information-only page (yes, those do still exist), you need a privacy policy.

WHY? Because you are collecting personal information. EVERY website that collects personal information must have a privacy policy. WHY? Because the European Union's (EU) General Data Protection Regulations (GDPR) & the California Consumer Privacy Act (CCPA) require it! You can't prevent someone from California or the EU from entering information on your website. The minute they do, those laws kick in. Your website visitors have the right to know what information you collect, why you collect it, whether and how you share it, and how they can get it removed from your database.

At this point the GDPR is the gold standard as the strictest, most inclusive consumer privacy regulation. California followed with the CCPA, but in the 2020 election cycle they passed the California Privacy Rights Act (CPRA). The CPRA is effective January 1, 2023, and applies to any information collected on or after January 1, 2022. It expands the consumer rights under the CCPA to include new rights and many more GDPR-like provisions, including the creation of a new regulator—the California Privacy Protection Agency, which will focus solely on the enforcement this new legislation. So, if you thought that being a U.S. based company meant you could safely ignore GDPR regulations, think again. Those regulations now exist on our shores!

The fines for ignoring these laws are stiff. CCPA **penalties currently run from $2500 to $7500 per violation.** Consumer data privacy legislation bills were considered in thirty states and Puerto Rico in 2020 (Source: NCSL.org). This is a big growth area, so it is only a matter of time before most states have enacted some form of consumer privacy laws. In other words, at some point your business will need this—don't wait.

Since the GDPR is the standard to meet (for now) so that you know your website is compliant everywhere, we'll focus on those provisions. Let's discuss what you need to know about GDPR. GDPR became effective on May 25, 2018. It was the first consumer privacy regulation to put stringent requirements on business owners with respect to the use of consumer personal data. GDPR is technology neutral – meaning it covers data you collect both online and offline, regardless of what device you use – computers, phones, cash registers, even paper. GDPR covers both data privacy AND data security, so it's not just what data you are collecting and how you use it, but also how you are protecting it, and how you will respond in the event of a data breach incident.

The data covered includes:

- **Personal Data.** Name, address, birth date, SSN.
- **Web Data.** Geolocation, IP address, cookie data.
- **Protected Data.** Health, biometrics, race/ethnicity, politics, sexual orientation.

The GDPR is not company location specific or company size specific. All businesses, regardless of location or size, are expected to comply with GDPR if:

- You collect personal information from EU citizens (newsletter, lead magnet, contact form); OR
- You sell goods or services to EU citizens; OR

- You use analytics on your website that can capture the browsing behavior of EU citizens.

It doesn't matter if you actually do business in the EU or you actively target EU consumers—if you are getting their personal information or analytics, GDPR applies.

Note: EU also has a "cookie notice" law in place, separate from GDPR. If you are actively targeting EU citizens, you'll need to separate your cookie policy from your privacy policy and post it separately on your website. Cookies are a small data file placed on your visitor's computer that allows you to distinguish that visitor from other users of your website. Users must be informed about the use of cookies on your site, what they track, the purpose, and must give their consent to allow you to retain the data captured via cookies.

Three GDPR definitions you need to know:

- **Data Subject.** The website visitor who provides their personal information.
- **Data Controller.** YOU, the website/business owner.
- **Data Processor.** The platform you are using to collect data. As a data controller, you likely have several data processors —your analytics/metrics provider, your email platform, your scheduler, your payment processor. The more services you use, the more processors you need to keep track of.

PENALTIES FOR NON-COMPLIANCE. PENALTIES CAN BE UP TO 20M Euro (in excess of $23M) or 4% of annual earnings, whichever is greater PLUS the potential of compensation owed to the data subjects whose personal information has been compromised. However, those amounts are discretionary and subject to the nature and magnitude of the violation. You are more likely to be given a warning and time to correct a violation than a fine for the first offense.

How to Comply

- Make sure your site is **httpS certified** (the "s" stands for security certification).
- **Do a data audit.** Know where your data comes from, where it is stored, how it is processed, how long it is kept, and how secure it is. Data audits should include your own computers, your paper files, any cloud-based storage and all your vendors, such as Google Analytics, email marketing platforms, and payment processing platforms.
- **Maintain a "Reasonable" level of data protection & privacy**, ensuring storage of data is secure, only the data you really need is collected, and data is stored no longer than necessary to fulfill the purpose for which consent is given.
- Have a **Posted Privacy Policy.**
- **Obtain Clear Consent** for all data collection. Switch from opt-out to opt-in procedures. Don't pre-check consent boxes. Make sure each consent form includes a link to your privacy policy.
- Have a **Breach Protocol Policy** in place so that you know how to respond in the event of a data breach and can meet the seventy-two-hour reporting requirement. Because reporting is state or nation specific in terms of requirements, your reporting obligations will depend on where your data subjects reside. Assuming your data subjects reside all over the world, you'll need to comply with the most stringent reporting requirements applicable.
- **Respond to requests** from data subjects for access to, correction of, or deletion of their information within thirty days.
- **Designate an EU Representative.** The likelihood that a small business will actually need this is slim, but you can look for companies that provide this as a service.

The EU directives you don't have to comply with as a small business:

- Maintaining a record or log of risks and compliance progress and processing activities only if >250 employees; and
- Appointing a data protection officer (DPO) for your company for "large volume" processing of personal data. Unfortunately, "large volume" is not defined in the GDPR. If you are processing large volumes of personal data, you are required to publish contact information for your DPO in your privacy policy. For smaller companies, simply naming a privacy officer is likely sufficient (that can be you!).

BREACH PROTOCOL. SINCE THE GDPR REQUIRES YOU TO have a breach protocol in place, it makes sense to discuss that policy next. Hacking and data breaches are an unfortunate reality in our world. Having a breach protocol in place *before* your website or computer is hacked and sensitive client information is compromised means you'll know precisely how to respond when disaster strikes. Don't wait until you're in an emergency situation to create your plan. You'll need to know the response requirements for your industry and jurisdiction, as well as the response requirements for any jurisdictions where you do business or have customers that could be affected by a breach. Your plans should include who you need to contact, what the time limitation is, and the methods of contact. Determine how you will handle press inquiries and social media posts.

WEBSITE DISCLAIMERS. IF YOUR BUSINESS DELVES INTO nutrition, physical fitness, wellness, or health in any form, you'll want a disclaimer that clearly states that you are not a licensed physician, dietician, etc. (unless you are, in which case disclose your certifica-tions), you do not diagnose or treat medical conditions, and that any fitness, wellness or nutrition plan should be undertaken in conjunc-tion with consultation with the client's physician. You want it displayed prominently, not hidden in the middle of your "About" page. This disclaimer is a protection for you in the event the client claims that your advice caused them any physical or mental harm. You've made it clear that they shouldn't undertake your program without consulting their doctor first. If you are in any of the professional fields of law, medicine, accounting, architecture, engineering, etc. you'll want a disclaimer that limits the information provided on your website to educational and informational use only and not profes-sional advice.

WEBSITE TERMS OF USE (ALSO KNOWN AS TERMS OF Service or Terms and Conditions). This policy governs the use of your website by a visitor. It is the terms they agree to in exchange for access to and use of the information or services available on your website.

There are two types of Terms of Use. The first is a "browser wrap" agreement. This is generally set up via a hyperlink in the footer of your website that leads to the page where your Terms of Use policy is housed. This is a passive form of agreement and best employed with websites that are information only and do not allow any user content or interaction. The second is a "click wrap" agreement. This is gener-ally deployed via a pop-up screen that requires your user to check that they have read and agreed to the Terms of Use. Because the click wrap agreement actively places the Terms of Use in front of your user, it provides stronger protection in the event of a later dispute and is best employed with websites that have any user interaction such as subscription-based sites, sites that allow user commenting and uploading of material (blogs, forums, etc.), online classrooms, and the like.

In the U.S., Terms of Use are not legally required. While you NEED a Privacy Policy to be compliant with regulations, there are no regulations mandating that your website post a Terms of Use policy.

Before you check out on this one, let's discuss some reasons you may WANT to have a Terms of Use policy on your website:

1. To disclaim liability for things like errors in the website content, performance and uptime of the website, malware and viruses, user posted content, or linked content.
2. To establish jurisdiction, venue, choice of law, and dispute resolution provisions. For more on what these provisions mean, revisit our discussion on contract provisions in chapter on contracts.
3. To protect your intellectual property rights to the content on your site. Possibly (depending on your business model) to provide licenses to your users for the content and establish the limitations of their license.
4. To regulate when and how others are permitted to link to your website.
5. To define permitted and prohibited conduct on your website – this can cover everything from using data to spam others, uploading viruses or other harmful content, and bullying, to copyright infringement, and more.

TERMS OF USE ARE MOST COMMONLY USED WHEN YOUR website has a subscription-based interface where users log in with a username and password. In this case, the Terms of Use are the rules of engagement for your website—how the website and the materials may and may not be used. But even if you don't have a subscription inter-face, a Terms of Use policy may be useful if you have any form of ecommerce (online ordering capability) to establish payment processes, return and refund policy, etc. or if you allow commenting on your website (such as on blog posts), to establish ownership and set the rules for commenting.

When drafting your own Terms of Use policy, don't simply copy and paste from someone else's website! First of all, it's copyright infringement. And if that isn't enough disincentive, unless you have the legal knowledge, you don't know if the Terms of Use policy you are cribbing from actually covers the needs of YOUR business. Do get help from an experienced small business attorney to ensure that your website Terms of Use policy covers the legal protections your business needs and is compliant with federal and state regulations where you are located. Periodically review your Terms of Use policy to ensure that it is up to date and accurately reflects your business' operating policies and procedures.

 Pro Tip: Website Terms of Use are NOT a substitute for a client services agreement or other contract with your clients or customers. It does not apply to services provided outside your website. It may apply to the e-commerce aspects of selling goods and services online, but only if you specifically call it out and link to your Terms of Use somewhere in the buying process. If you do this, it is best to use a click wrap agreement, rather than a browser wrap agreement.

DIGITAL MILLENNIUM COPYRIGHT ACT (DMCA)

If your website allows consumer generated content you need this provision! I'm a serious DMCA evangelist. Wait a minute! *What is DMCA?* The Digital Millennium Copyright Act is a 1998 U.S. federal law that addresses the protection of copyrighted materials online. The Act provides a Safe Harbor provision for websites that passively host user generated content, 17 U.S.C. §512. Because copyright infringement damages can range **up to $150,000 per work**, every website owner that hosts content provided by others needs the protection afforded by the DMCA Safe Harbor.

- **What is User Generated Content?** If your website hosts guest blog posts, allows comments on your blog posts, allows customer reviews, if you have a forum on your site that allows user communication, if users can upload photos, documents, or video to your website—these are all examples of user generated content. If these things are added to your site without you first reviewing and approving it, then you are passively hosting user generated content.

- **How does this apply to you as a small business owner?** If any portion of your website content is user generated content, the DMCA Safe Harbor protects YOU from what they post. Normally, if a user of your website posts a copyrighted photo or other copyrighted material, under copyright law, you are liable for copyright infringement for permitting that photo or other copyrighted material to appear on your website.

"But that's not fair!" you say. You don't have any control over what your users post. You are absolutely right. It's <u>not</u> fair. Unfortunately, it's the law. Copyright infringement is a strict liability offense (meaning you don't have to know you are infringing to be liable). The copyright protection agencies (Getty, PicRights, Pixabay, Picsy, etc.) are in business to protect the rights of the photographers creating those photos. Those agencies don't care that you aren't the one who originally posted that photo of the Brooklyn Bridge that some user "borrowed" from the Internet. That photo on your website is their bread and butter. Luckily for you, there is an easy and very inexpensive way to avoid liability. DMCA Safe Harbor to the rescue!

How does DMCA Safe Harbor work?

The rationale for the Safe Harbor is that a website that passively allows user generated content is a mere conduit that should be provided immunity because they do not *actively* engage in infringing activities. Only websites that aggregate content in a non-selective manner are eligible for DMCA Safe Harbor protection.

In order to qualify for Safe Harbor protection, you must meet all of the following criteria:

- You are not aware of the infringing material on your website;
- Once infringing materials are brought to your attention, you expeditiously take down the infringing material;
- You do not gain any direct financial benefit from the infringing material;
- You designate an agent for receipt of copyright infringement claims, both on your website and by registering with the U.S. Copyright Office;
- You manage and implement a notice and takedown procedure. This procedure must be posted on your website via a standalone link or within your Terms of Use; and
- You adopt and implement a repeat infringer policy.

How do I get DMCA Safe Harbor Protection?

1. Create an account at the U.S. Copyright Office. Refer to the Resources chapter for the link to register.
2. Determine who will act as your agent. Your agent can be an individual, a specific position or department within your company, or even a third-party provider, such as your website manager. Your designated agent must act expeditiously on any take down notification.
3. After completing Step 1, designate your agent with the U.S. Copyright Office. The cost to register your designated agent is currently just $6. It's the cheapest form of government sponsored insurance you can buy! Refer to the Resources chapter for links to instructions to designate an agent and to provide your designation.
4. Create and post your DMCA notice on your website. While examples are available on many websites, don't just copy and paste someone else's policy. First, that's copyright infringement. Second, you want your policy to reflect how

you will actually operate to enforce DMCA provisions. If you aren't sure how to craft your DMCA notice, consult with your attorney. Some websites have stand-alone DMCA links, while others have imbedded their DMCA notice in their Terms of Use.

MY DMCA NOTICE IS ACTIVE. NOW WHAT?

With the DMCA notice in place, if you receive notification of allegedly infringing material on your website, you must immediately investigate and remove the infringing materials from your website. Then you can notify the party who contacted you that you've removed the infringing material. Your prompt action to ensure that the infringing materials are taken down fulfills your duties under the DMCA and should resolve any claim by a third party.

But be warned—The DMCA Safe Harbor does not protect you from liability for infringing material that you post yourself! Always make sure you own the copyright to any material you post or have obtained permission from the copyright owner.

I am aware of one unfortunate business owner who found this out the hard way. She "borrowed" a photo she found online that fit her website needs but didn't get a license or permission to use it. She figured that as a small business it wouldn't be noticed. She was wrong. The next thing she knew, she had a demand letter from Getty Images and had to pay thousands of dollars for her use of the photo.

EMAIL MARKETING POLICIES

Did you know that even your email marketing and newsletter list is subject to regulation? Well, it is! And depending on where you market, you may need to know about the laws of more than one country or state when it comes to email marketing. Here's an over-view of three major pieces of legislation that will provide a start to

your understanding of the regulations governing your email
marketing.

- The U.S. anti-spam legislation, the CAN-SPAM Act, was
  designed to slow down the amount of spam email arriving
  in the inboxes of Americans. But the consumer protection it
  provides is limited because it is an *opt-out* law. What this
  means is that ANYONE can send you a marketing email,
  whether they have a relationship with you or not, whether
  they have your permission or not, as long as they provide a
  clear way within the email for you to opt-out of receiving
  any future email from them.
- Canada's Anti-Spam Legislation (CASL) is Canada's version
  of our CAN-SPAM law. Canada has an affirmative *opt-IN*
  requirement. CASL covers both email and text messages.
  Which means you can't send anyone in Canada a marketing
  (advertising) email or text message unless they have
  affirmatively opted in to receive your communications.
  CASL has been in effect since 2015. According to the
  Canadian Government website, this legislation resulted in a
  37% decrease in spam email in its first year. That's an
  impressive statistic showing the value of requiring
  permission for email marketing.[1]
- The GDPR (discussed in detail earlier in this chapter) also
  requires affirmative *opt-IN* for email marketing.

In fact, almost every nation that has email marketing legislation,
other than the U.S., requires affirmative opt-IN. What do you do if
you have a mixed list? Or if you don't know where your newsletter
sign-ups are from? The bottom line is that the spam laws don't care
where your company is located. They care about where you are
sending the email. You must be compliant with the laws of the recipient's country or state.

Pro Tip: If you comply with the most stringent regulations out there, you will generally be covered for all the regulations. As of the writing of this book, GDPR has the most stringent regulations with respect to email marketing, and in fact, all data use. Remember, GDPR requires affirmative, informed consent specific to each data use. To comply, you want to have a consent checkbox for EVERY form on your website that requests personal information—your email list sign-up for your mailing list or newsletter, contact forms for your CRM, and forms to receive any free materials should all have the checkbox. Boxes cannot be pre-checked! And each form should link to your privacy policy.

CAN-SPAM COMPLIANCE

This book is geared to small businesses within the United States, so we can't skip digging into the legislation that is arguably most relevant to your email marketing. Although CAN-SPAM is separate legislation from consumer privacy protection, they really do go hand-in-hand. The privacy legislation requires that you take certain steps to inform visitors and protect their personal information when you collect it on your website. What you are collecting is typically names and email addresses (along with metrics) to use in your email marketing efforts.

Do you use email marketing in your business? (I'm pretty much assuming you do!) Would you like to avoid tens of thousands in fines? Then pay attention because you will want to be sure that you are compliant with this law! Under the CAN-SPAM Act, **each individual email is subject to penalties up to $43,280**!

CAN-SPAM is an acronym for Controlling the Assault of Non-Solicited Pornography and Marketing and was signed into law in the U.S. by President George W. Bush in December 2003. It was designed to slow down the amount of unsolicited junk email showing up in your inbox.

The Act accomplished three things:

- Established national standards for the sending of commercial e-mail;
- Gave recipients the right to have senders stop emailing them; and
- Set forth TOUGH penalties for violations.

The Act is enforced by the Federal Trade Commission (FTC). According to the FTC website, in 2016 the FTC raised the penalties for violations from $16K to over $40K and have had several increases since then, bringing the penalty to its current level. [2]

Despite its name, the CAN-SPAM Act doesn't apply just to bulk email. It covers all commercial email. The law defines commercial email as *"any electronic mail message the primary purpose of which is the commercial advertisement or promotion of a commercial product or service."* That's a lot of "commercial" but what it boils down to is this: if your intent in sending the email is to make money, even indirectly, then you need to comply with the Act.

In addition to commercial email, the CAN-SPAM Act recognizes two other types of email. Transactional email is an email sent regarding a product or service the customer has already purchased. For example, a notification that the order has shipped. Relationship email is intended to build your relationship with your email list, such as a newsletter. If you combine commercial and relationship content in a single email, I recommend erring on the side of caution and making sure it is can-spam compliant!

Being in compliance with the law isn't complicated. Below is a list of CAN-SPAM's main requirements sourced directly from the guidance on the FTC website.

1. **Don't use false or misleading header information.** The "From," "To," "Reply-To," and routing information, including the originating domain name and email address

must be accurate and identify the person or business who initiated the message.

2. **Don't use deceptive subject lines.** The subject line must accurately reflect the content of the message. While it is fun to get clever with subject lines that entice your reader to open the email, make sure the subject line actually relates to the information in the email. If your subject line is "I have a secret," your message content needs to talk about that secret!

3. **Admit that it's advertising.** The law gives you a lot of leeway in how to do this, but you must disclose clearly and conspicuously that your message is an advertisement. This can be as simple as placing text at the bottom of the email saying, "This advertisement was sent by (your business name here)."

4. **Provide a physical address.** Your message must include a valid physical postal address. This can be your current street address, a post office box you've registered with the U.S. Postal Service, or a private mailbox you've registered with a commercial mail agency.

5. **Tell recipients how to opt out.** Your message must include a clear, conspicuous, and simple way for the recipient to opt out of your email list. Provide a return email address or an easy internet-based opt-out form. You may create a menu to allow a recipient to opt out of certain types of messages, but it must include the option to stop all commercial messages from you. Make sure your spam filter doesn't block these opt-out requests.

6. **Handle opt-out requests promptly.** The opt-out mechanism you employ must honor a recipient's opt-out request within ten business days. You can't charge a fee, require any personally identifying information beyond an email address, or make the recipient take any step other than sending a reply email or visiting a single page on an Internet website as a

condition for honoring an opt-out request. Once someone has opted out, you can't sell or transfer their email addresses, with the sole exception of sharing the addresses with a company you've hired to help you comply with the CAN-SPAM Act.

7. **Monitor what others are doing on your behalf.** Even if you hire a company to handle your email marketing, you can't contract away your legal responsibility to comply with the law. Both your company and the company that is actually sending the message may be held legally responsible.

Remember, as we discussed earlier, under the CAN-SPAM Act each individual email is subject to penalties up to $43,280 so you want to make sure your email marketing is compliant!

OPERATIONAL POLICIES

Operational Policies refer generally to internal company policies that govern the day-to-day activities of your small business. I can't stress enough how important your operational policies are to your success. As Jeff Platt, CEO of Sky Zone said: "Spend time up front to invest in systems and processes to make long-term growth sustainable."

Depending on your industry, there may be many more policies that you need than you'll find discussed here. My intention isn't to be all-inclusive, but to provide representative policies that most small businesses are likely to need. In this section we will briefly discuss refund policies and employee-related policies, then we will take a deeper dive into document and email retention policies.

REFUND AND RETURN POLICIES

Have your return and refund policies established before you start selling and apply it consistently across all customers and clients. If you are product based, post your return policy at the register for physical locations and at check-out for online transactions, and include it in your Terms of Use online. Don't make it hard for your customers to find this information! If your refund policy is readily visible it is harder for a customer to claim they were unaware, and consequently, easier for you to enforce. If you are a service-based business, include your refund policy in your client services contracts and on your website Terms of Use.

EMPLOYEE RELATED POLICIES

When you get to the point of having W-2 employees, you'll need a host of employee related policies. Consider having an employee handbook drafted that pulls all of these policies together in one cohesive document. The standard legally required policies will include statements about equal employment opportunity, discrimination/inclusion, sexual harassment, bullying and violence, and non-retaliation. Additionally, you'll want clear statements about attendance requirements and paid time off, dress code, alcohol and drug use, and other office/plant/warehouse conduct, information technology rules such as expectation of privacy on company servers, use of personal devices for company work, social media policies, etc. If you provide benefits such as medical and retirement, a simple statement in the employee handbook referring them to benefit documentation will suffice. Adding specific information about medical and retirement benefits can be problematic as those benefits can change from year to year. Keeping the statement high level alleviates the need to revise your employee manual every year. That said, the employee manual should be reviewed annually just to ensure that all of your policies are still in play and being enforced. If policies have changed, the manual should be updated.

 Pro Tip: Don't have your manuals coil bound. Use three-ring binders that allow you to replace only those pages where information has been updated. That will save you on having to reprint the entire manual when you make policy changes!

Document Retention and Destruction

The businesses that will do best in the long run are those that establish processes early on to handle, keep track of, and maintain order in their paperwork. Even if you are a paper-free environment, you still have paperwork. It's just electronic. And it still needs to be organized and maintained so you can find what you need, when you need it, and know you are not missing any important documents. The Document Retention and Destruction policy deals with the systematic review, retention, and destruction of documents created or received in the ordinary course of business. It includes both paper and electronic documents. It includes both structured (contracts, corporate records, purchase orders, bank statements) and unstructured (email, instant messaging, text messaging, handwritten notes) documents.

I *could* write an entire book devoted to document retention and destruction. For a large business, it can be a complicated, time-consuming, onerous project to create a document retention and destruction policy. In fact, in my role as General Counsel, we engaged an outside company to map all of our documents and help us understand what documents were being created, by whom, and where they were being stored. The process to create our initial document retention policy took over six months! For your small business, you have less people creating and receiving documents, so it will hopefully be a little easier to pin down.

First, you need to identify each type of document created and/or received in the normal course of your business. Let me help you get started:

Business Formation and Planning

- Articles of Organization or Incorporation
- Operating Agreement or Bylaws
- Corporate Minutes

- Ownership Certificates
- Tax ID Number
- Tax elections
- Business Plan
- Mission/Vision/Values Statement
- Insurance policies
- Licenses and permits

TRANSACTIONAL

- Contracts
- Emails
- Proposals for your clients
- Lease agreements
- Vendor agreements

OPERATIONAL/FACILITIES

- Equipment manuals
- Leases
- Warranties
- Utilities (gas, electric, water/sewer, phone, internet)
- Software necessary to run your business
- Policies and documented procedures

HUMAN RESOURCES

- Employment or Independent Contractor agreements
- Tax forms (W-2s, W-9s, 1099s)

- Employment applications and resumes
- NDA/Confidentiality agreements
- Employee manual and policies
- Organizational chart
- Performance evaluations
- Job descriptions
- Metrics
- Benefits information (medical, 401K, Paid Time Off)

FINANCIAL

- Bookkeeping records
- Invoices
- Receipts
- Credit card statements
- Bank records
- Tax returns

MARKETING

- Client roster
- Potential client information
- Marketing copy
- Website copy
- Articles
- Email campaigns
- Blog posts
- Brochures
- Business cards
- Facebook business page
- LinkedIn profile

- Other social media
- Books
- Class and course materials
- Videos
- Podcasts

ONCE YOU HAVE A LAUNDRY LIST OF ALL YOUR DOCUMENTS, you need to identify any legal requirements for how long you MUST retain records for your business.

Is there a state or federal requirement for retention? In the financial and employment categories there are a host of statutes defining requirement periods. Just by way of a few examples, some accounting records, like bank statements, should be retained for three years, while others, like payroll records, should be retained for seven years, and some, such as cash books and charts of accounts should be retained permanently. Employee applications should be retained for three years, employee personnel records should be retained for seven years after an employee is no longer with the company, but information about IRA/Keogh plans should be retained permanently. Confusing? Yes. Check with your attorney or accountant to determine which of the myriad of regulatory requirements for retention apply to you.

If there is no statutorily required retention period, what is the applicable statute of limitations for actions which might require these documents? This can vary by state, but by way of example, the statute of limitations for breach of contract in many states is two years. That means you should retain copies of your contracts for **at least** two years after the contract has been completed. Finally, you should consider industry best practices and your own business needs. What is the likelihood that you will refer back to this document at some point in the future?

Your document retention policy should address retention periods for each category of documents and should also address plans for document destruction. Once you have the policy mapped out, you need a procedure in place to actually carry out your policy. When will you destroy documents? Set a regular schedule for this activity. How will you destroy documents? Sensitive documents should not just be tossed in the trash, they should be shredded. Plan to purchase a shredder or utilize a shredding service.

Why? Why go to all of this trouble?

1. **Business Efficiency**. With a solid document retention and destruction policy in place, you know what documents you have and where they are stored. Small businesses that ran a tight ship were on top of their records and were able to quickly pull needed information and apply for Paycheck Protection Program loans during the COVID pandemic. Those that weren't on top of their records had a harder time pulling together the information needed for the loan application and many missed out on the opportunity.

2. **Litigation Protection**. A legally defensible retention policy, consistently applied, provides a shield for you against claims of spoliation (claims that you purposefully got rid of evidence) in a lawsuit. It also saves you a lot of worry and hassle in the event the IRS audits your tax return. You will know you have all of the supporting documentation neatly filed away and accessible.

3. **Compliance**. You'll have the peace of mind of knowing that you are legally compliant with all statutes and regulations applicable to your business.

4. **Cost**. Generally, the less you retain, the less it will cost if you are sued. Document production in response to a subpoena or discovery request is very expensive. Your retention policy can save you a ton of money and aggravation in the event of a lawsuit or subpoena for your records.

As you can see, it behooves every business to have an established policy and procedure for handling document retention and destruction. There are a lot of down-the-line benefits to setting this up early in your business endeavors.

EMAIL RETENTION POLICY

A special note on **email** which, together with instant messaging and text messaging, is the single most problematic area for document retention and destruction. So much so, that email warrants its own section in addressing the problems it can wreak for the unwary.

Why you ask? Here are my top three reasons:

1. **Lack of Deletion.** We fail to make regular deletion a habit. Email piles up in your inbox and pretty soon you are using the search feature to find anything. Email needs to be cleaned out in the same way that paper files do! You should regularly schedule deletion of email as a business activity.

2. **Informality.** We treat email (and text and instant messaging) very informally. People will say things in email that they wouldn't say in a formal letter sent via postal mail. But there's the rub: in the world of litigation, it's the same thing. Whether it is a formal typed letter on company letterhead, or a quick email, it has the exact same evidentiary value in litigation.

3. **The Smoking Gun.** Email is where litigators look first for the smoking gun—that one piece of evidence that can win their case. See number two to answer the question why. Unfortunately, case law bears out the value of email in litigation and companies have lost thousands and even millions of dollars because of ill-advised email content.

Now you are thinking, well, Cheri, what's the big deal if the litigation attorney wants my email? I'm careful and I don't say anything in email that would potentially make waves! Good question. The answer is simple: **COST.**

Back in 2012, as General Counsel, I was tasked with creating my company's document retention and destruction policy. At that time the eDiscovery cost for producing and reviewing email was estimated at roughly $5.00 PER EMAIL. According to the Rand Institute for Civil Justice, roughly 73% of the cost of eDiscovery is attorney review. Thankfully, Artificial Intelligence has brought down the initial cost of gathering and parsing email to weed out documents that are entirely irrelevant to the discovery request or the subpoena for your records. But you still need attorney review for the remainder of the email that could potentially be relevant. The attorney review is designed to determine:

1. Is the email relevant to the discovery request? If not, it doesn't have to be produced.
2. If the email is relevant, is there any reason to exclude it from production? Reasons can include attorney/client privilege, trade secret, sensitive client material, and more.

There are attorneys and eDiscovery services that specialize in this kind of review. At the low end of the cost spectrum, you can probably get through discovery for about $2.50 per email. If you have 200 emails in your inbox, that's $500 in review costs. Go ahead and look at how many emails are in your inbox—if you've been in business for a few years and don't regularly delete email, it is probably in the thousands. If you have employees and check the number company-wide, it's more likely in the tens of thousands or more. Ten thousand emails will cost $25,000 in discovery review! And that is calculated at the low end of the cost spectrum.

In addition, you have lost opportunity cost. The time you spend gathering, sorting, and flagging emails for potential issues of concern is time away from your business and income producing activity.

To help you avoid getting sucked into the email vortex, here are eight tips to reduce the amount of email you retain and the amount of potentially discoverable and relevant material in email:

1. **Treat all email as public documents.** This should go

without saying, but don't put anything in an email that you wouldn't want your dear grandmother to read. And if your grandmother happens to be a feisty old broad who swears like a sailor and is impossible to embarrass, then don't put anything in email that you wouldn't want read out loud in a courtroom in front of a jury and witnesses or printed on the front page of a newspaper. Because, YES, it happens! Give email the formality it deserves as the current replacement for a formal letter on company letterhead.

2. **Send links, not attachments**. For example, I want to share a document with three other staff. I send an email with the document attached. The email is 70Kb. Sent to three staff, I have consumed 280Kb of storage on the email server and have four copies of that business record residing in email. Conversely, I send a link to the document where it resides on the company hard drive or to a Dropbox (or similar) account to the same three staff. The email is now only 5Kb, taking up a total of 20Kb of storage space and zero copies of the business record in email! That's a 1400% reduction in storage space. Multiply that over the number of emails sent in a day and maybe you can stop buying additional hard drives and servers once you put this procedure into place.

3. **Limit your audience**. We all have a bad habit of hitting "reply all." In some cases, it is a CYA maneuver, but often it is just reflex. Think twice before hitting "reply all." Does the whole company need to see this? Or is my audience really only one person? Only send email to those who need to see it. For example, in a group email if someone says something that you think is very witty and you want to let them know, when you reply to say, "Thanks for the witty comment," replying to just the sender is sufficient. No need to generate multiple emails and give everyone else one more message to delete!

4. **Step away from the computer**. Not all messages are suitable for email. Are you discussing sensitive information?

Is your subject something difficult to explain? Sometimes picking up the phone or taking a walk down the hall to speak in person may be a better alternative.

5. **Keep it short and sweet.** Whenever possible, email should be short and sweet. Five sentences max. If it takes more than five sentences to make your point, perhaps email isn't the best choice for that particular communication. See # 4 – Step away from the computer.

6. **Don't let business records live in email.** Documents that rise to the level of a "business record" (documents you need to retain for compliance purposes or business needs) should NOT be saved in email. Final drafts of contracts, newsletters, blog posts, marketing campaigns, news stories, help docs, reports, minutes, etc. should be saved to your computer's hard drive. Once a document is finalized, all draft versions should be deleted from both email and your hard drive.

7. **Unsubscribe.** Stem the tide of incoming email by unsubscribing from email sources you don't read such as mailing lists, industry publications, or anything else you originally subscribed to but are no longer interested in receiving. I can't recommend "unsubscribe" for SPAM email as that action just seems to increase the SPAM. For those items, set up rules or filters in your email program to send the spam directly to your junk or deleted items folders.

8. **DELETE, DELETE, DELETE!** Seriously folks, learn where the delete key is on your keyboard and use it liberally! **The delete key is your new best friend.** Of course, you need to delete in accordance with your retention policy. But for the love of all things holy, do not set a long retention period for email. As General Counsel, I had set a retention period of one week for transitory email (meeting set-up, cake in the kitchen, co-worker leaving, etc.) and thirty days for all other email that didn't rise to the level of business records (things you have to keep for compliance or business needs). This

forced employees to regularly delete email. But it kept company server capacity lower and the risk of astronomical eDiscovery costs was effectively mitigated. Email to set up meetings? Delete it when the meeting is over! Email from news lists? Read and delete. If you aren't reading it, unsubscribe. Spam? Block and delete. Transactional email that rises to the level of business records (something you need to keep for retention compliance or business needs)? If it is an attachment, save that to the appropriate folder on your hard drive (see #6) and delete it from the email. If it is email text, save it to a clearly labeled folder so it is segregated and easily located if/when the need arises.

 Pro Tip: Don't forget to empty your deleted items folder! You can make this a daily or weekly habit—set an appointment on your calendar to remind yourself. Or use the features of your email service to set up automatic emptying of the deleted items folder when you exit the email program, or on another regular basis that works for your needs.

KEY TAKEAWAYS

- Your website NEEDS a Privacy Policy.
- Your email marketing should be compliant with the CAN-SPAM Act.
- Having a solid document retention and destruction policy is beneficial for audits, litigation, and rapid response when something happens to rock the boat.
- Email deserves special attention in your internal policy efforts.

7

YOUR BRAND IDENTITY

Your personal brand serves as your best protection
against business factors you can't control.
Dan Schawbel

*B*oat, crew, provisions—what's left? No self-respecting captain would launch her boat without a proper naming ceremony!

When it comes to your business, you may spend a lot of time choosing a name, colors, a clever tagline, and designing a logo. These pieces of your business are your brand identity. Which shouldn't be confused with your brand or your branding. Your brand is the sum total of the perceptions, opinions, feelings, and thoughts that your customers or clients have about you, your service, and your business. Your branding is the action driven process that builds awareness and brand reputation—it is the emotional bridge between you and your ideal client. Branding encompasses things like sending out an email newsletter, posting on social media, engaging in an advertising campaign. These are the tactics and strategies you employ to gain forward momentum, increase recognition, and close more sales.

Your brand identity is a form of intellectual property (IP). And when it comes to IP, the mistakes made most often by entrepreneurs include infringing others IP and failing to protect their own IP.

The fifth key to launching a legally sound business is protecting your intellectual property. Let's talk briefly about the types of IP.

1. A **Trademark** protects a word, phrase, symbol, and/or design that identifies and distinguishes the source of a physical product.
2. A **Service mark** protects a word, phrase, symbol, and/or design that identifies and distinguishes the source of a service.
3. **Copyright** arises automatically upon creation and protects original works of authorship fixed in a tangible medium including literary, dramatic, musical, and artistic works.
4. **Patents** protect novel inventions through registration with the United States Patent and Trademark Office (USPTO). Filing for a patent is a lengthy and often costly (think in terms of three to five years and potentially tens or hundreds of thousands dollars) undertaking and should not be attempted without the aid of an attorney who specializes in patents in your specific industry. As I have limited experience with patents, I'll leave this topic to other experts.
5. **Trade Secrets** protect the "secret sauce" of your business, such as the formula for Coca Cola or Kentucky Fried Chicken. Trade secrets can also protect things like customer lists, computer code, algorithms, sales data, and more. Trade secret intellectual property rights are secured simply by taking precautions to ensure the secret remains secret, such as through limited disclosure and NDA's for those who are given access. Trade secrets are also beyond the scope of this book.

Now that you know what IP is, let's talk about why you should care.

TRADEMARKS AND SERVICE MARKS

Before you spend your first dime developing your brand identity with your new name, logo, and tagline, put on the brakes! You need to make sure your intended brand identity isn't already being used by someone else in your industry. You don't want to get your business up and running and build a customer base, only to have to start over because you've received a Cease-and-Desist letter from an unhappy trademark owner whose mark you've infringed. You could spend thousands of dollars setting up a website, printing business cards and brochures, purchasing domain names, heck, even printing company-branded polo shirts, only to have to ditch it all, pay over any profits you've made to date to the trademark owner, and start from scratch. This precise scenario has bankrupted many a small business!

Brand Identity assets must be researched before you adopt them. As an example, when thinking about my own brand identity, I came up with several name ideas for my law practice that excited me: Inside Out Legal, Beacon Law, and North Star Legal were names I considered. Each idea was my own original thought (usually from a dream). It wasn't that I saw it on a website and simply wanted to co-opt it. But each time I researched the potential marks, I discovered other attorneys, often in my own state, already using similar names in various forms. In each case, I abandoned the idea of using that name for my business because I knew there would be issues with getting a service mark. That wouldn't necessarily stop me from using the imagery in website copy—because the imagery itself isn't legally protected—but it will stop me from using one of those ideas as the NAME, LOGO, or TAGLINE for my business.

How do you research your potential brand identity ideas?

- Start with Google. What pops up in the results when you search for your intended name or tagline?

- Search social media platforms. Is someone on Facebook or Instagram using the name or tagline you wanted? As we will discuss shortly, they may have common law rights to that mark even if they haven't filed for trademark registration.
- Go to the USPTO website. Search for federal trademark registrations on your potential name or mark. Performing an appropriate search in TESS (the USPTO search platform) can be tricky, so you might want legal assistance with this one. Just because the *exact* name you want isn't listed on the trademark register doesn't mean there isn't a confusingly similar name (different spelling, an additional word, a different word but sounds the same) that would create a risk of trademark infringement or cause denial of your trademark application.
- Search state corporate or LLC records in the states where you plan to do business. Do other businesses already use the same or a similar name?
- Check out GoDaddy.com or other domain name registrars. Is the domain name you want available?

If this sounds like an onerous amount of work just to use a name, please rest assured, it IS! No matter how well you think you have searched, I feel quite confident in stating that you won't uncover half of the potential concerns that an IP attorney would. Trying to do this on your own can take valuable time away from your income producing activities and you may still miss something that an IP attorney would find. Investing in a professional trademark clearance search before you set up your entity and before you pay good money for a designer logo and website will be money well spent!

Short of hiring an attorney to do the search, if the .com version of your name is taken, this a huge red flag that someone else may already be using the mark. Don't make the mistake of assuming that you can just buy the .biz or .net version and you'll be fine. Because it's likely you won't. If you run into issues with your intended name or logo in these places, consider choosing a different name.

Once you've cleared your intended mark and started using it, you need to take steps to protect it! Filing for a trademark registration is one action step you can take to legally protect your brand.

For both trademark and service mark, you have **common law rights** to your mark as soon as you start using it in commerce. What does using it in commerce mean? It means you use the mark on a product, on your website, or on promotional brochures, etc. You can use the TM/SM designation even if you haven't filed an application for a trademark or service mark with the USPTO. Note that the TM/SM designators do not confer any specific legal rights or protections beyond notice to the public that you consider this mark to be your intellectual property and your presumed intent to file for a federal registration.

Federal registration of a trademark or service mark with the USPTO has several distinct advantages over reliance on your common law rights, including notice to the public that your mark is, in fact, registered with the USPTO, a legal presumption of ownership nation-wide, and the exclusive right to use your mark on or in connection with the goods or services set forth in the registration. Use the ® symbol once the USPTO has granted your application and your mark is considered registered.

So, go ahead and start using the $^{TM/SM}$ symbols to designate the marks you consider your IP assets as soon as you start using them in commerce. When your company has grown sufficiently and you have the budget for it, you may want to consider filing for a trademark or service mark for your brand assets with the USPTO.

What types of assets can be trademarked or service marked? Your business name, the name of any programs or classes, your business logo, your business tagline, even specific colors (Tiffany blue) or sounds (the NBC chimes) can potentially receive trademark protection. But to receive trademark protection a mark must in some way identify your company as the source of the product or service.

If you eventually hope to trademark your business name, logo, or tagline and want to build an intellectual property portfolio, there are a few things you should be aware of up front. Not all potential trademarks are created equal and the type of name or logo you choose may affect your ability to get a trademark registration with the USPTO.

WEAK TRADEMARKS

The weakest potential marks are those that are merely descriptive of your business. This includes descriptive words (dependable, best), surnames (Jones, Smith) and geographic locations (New York, Paris, American). For example: Accurate Accounting, Pisano's Pizza Place, or Flourtown Florist. These names tell you what the business is, sometimes including the name of the town it is located in or the name of the owner, but there is nothing distinctive about the name that would distinguish it from similar accounting firms, florists, or pizza shops. The USPTO doesn't allow any business to trademark generic names.

The only exceptions are when an owner can establish that consumers associate the mark with the owner's specific product or service. This is generally accomplished through a long period of established use, or substantial advertising and sales. Examples are Chap-Stick and McDonald's.

STRONG TRADEMARKS

Strong marks are unique, memorable, often made-up words. For example, "Google" and "Bing" as search engines. The words are entirely made up and have no actual connection to what the company does. They aren't merely descriptive. Other marks that are generally eligible for trademark are those where the meaning is completely arbitrary. Think Apple for computers and phones. The more unusual your name is, the more likely it will be eligible for trademark protection. Think outside the box! Of course, fanciful names come with a trade-off where your marketing is concerned because they don't clearly and conspicuously indicate who you are, what you do, and what problem you solve for your potential customers. Weigh the benefits of trademark against the additional marketing work when deciding on your name.

COPYRIGHT

Copyright protects original works of authorship fixed in a tangible medium, including literary, dramatic, musical, and artistic works. The protection covers the author's creative expression, but not the facts or ideas underlying that expression. For example, if you write a blog post comparing three different email marketing platforms, the facts, such as the names of the platforms, the features included, and the price, are NOT subject to copyright. Anyone can freely use that information. What is protected is the creative expression, such as the words you use to describe your experience with the platform, how it operates, and your arrangement of the compare and contrast or pros and cons information.

"Fixed in a tangible medium" means that you've taken the expression of your thoughts and ideas out of your head and recorded them in some manner. A photographic image exists on the drive of your camera or cell phone, a blog post or Facebook Live video exists as a file on your website page, a poem you wrote is recorded on paper or in a word processing file on your computer. These all qualify as being "fixed in a tangible medium."

How does all of this relate to your small business? Your marketing copy, website copy, blog posts, Facebook Live and Instagram videos, course content, and the eBook you wrote are all original works of authorship fixed in a tangible medium. They are all subject to copyright protection and you will want to take measures to ensure that your rights are protected. Your website should have a copyright notice in the footer that is updated yearly. Your copyright notice looks like this: © Your Company Name 2018 – 2021. You may also choose to register your copyright with the U.S. Copyright Office. Doing so provides additional protections that your common law copyright doesn't.

What happens if someone is infringing your copyright protected material? You have a few options. You can ignore it if you feel it is okay for anyone to use your material for their own benefit. You can send them a Cease-and-Desist letter, basically calling them out on the inappropriate use of your material and asking them to stop immediately. If the Cease-and-Desist letter isn't effective at curbing their bad behavior, the next step is a lawsuit.

BUT ... you must have your copyright registered with the U. S. Copyright Office before you are able to file a lawsuit. This is a relatively new wrinkle in copyright law. The federal circuit courts used to be divided on whether a registration was necessary and some allowed lawsuits to proceed on the strength of an application having been filed with the Copyright Office prior to the actual registration having issued. But in March of 2019, in the case of Fourth Estate Public Benefit Corp. v. Wall-Street.com LLC, the U.S. Supreme Court settled the split among the federal courts, holding that you must have a valid registration in order to pursue copyright infringement litigation.

What does this mean for your business? It means that for anything you are adamant about protecting, you will want to proactively file an application for copyright registration. Should you register every single blog post, photograph, video, and piece of content you create? Realistically, probably not. You can save time and money by filing quarterly registrations for a single filing fee for: groups of photographs; the text-only portions of website articles and blog posts; or unpublished podcast audio recordings. Most other content must be registered individually. But you definitely want to register your income producing content—just so unscrupulous and creatively lazy trolls can't come along and steal all your hard work in order to profit from it themselves!

As many small business owners I know are also authors, proactively filing for a copyright registration on your book (or other copyrightable material) can prove beneficial in another regard; if you file before the earlier of (1) 90 days from first publication, OR (2) before infringement begins (as opposed to waiting until you know of infringement) you are entitled to claim statutory damages. (Section 412 U.S. Copyright Act). The beauty of statutory damages is that it is an amount determined by the court without you having to prove ACTUAL damages. Statutory damages are usually between $750 and $30,000 per work but can be increased up to $150,000 per work if the infringement is shown to be intentional. Actual damages, on the other hand include profit that the copyright owner lost as a result of the infringement (for example, a license fee or royalty income) as well as any additional profits the infringer received as a result of the infringement. Actual damages are often difficult to prove (and the copyright holder has the burden of proof), so statutory damages save copyright owners from the task of providing evidence of actual damages. (Section 504 U.S. Copyright Act).

Copyright protection doesn't cover "fair use" which is defined in the Copyright Act as reproduction for purposes such as criticism, comment, news reporting, teaching, scholarship, or research. Use of your content for these specific purposes is not considered infringement of your rights as the copyright holder. In determining whether a use is "fair use" courts must consider all four of the following factors:

- The purpose and character of the use, including whether it is commercial or nonprofit. If the use is intended to make money, it probably won't qualify as fair use.
- The nature of the copyrighted work.
- The amount or substantiality of the portion used to the work as a whole. If the use quotes a single sentence from a 200-page book, it will lean in favor of fair use. If the use embodies a full page of a two-page magazine article, it probably won't be protected as fair use, unless the use is considered a parody.
- The effect of the use on the potential market or value of the copyrighted work. For example, if a photographer takes an iconic photo of the Brooklyn Bridge at sunset and plans to license it exclusively to *Time Magazine* for a tidy sum, the value of that photograph lies in the fact that it is, as yet, unpublished. If a hacker steals the photograph from the photographer's computer and sells poster size prints and greeting cards of that photograph on Amazon, the hacker has substantially diminished the potential market or value of the photograph for the copyright owner.

Protecting intellectual property assets is usually one of the last things on the "to do" list of small business owners, but it doesn't have to be that way. While filing for a trademark registration is costly, appropriately using the ^{TM} symbol is free! Copyright attaches automatically to your work that is eligible for copyright protection, but proactively filing for copyright registration is fairly inexpensive and can be quite valuable in the event infringement litigation becomes necessary. Likewise, taking the time (or spending the money) to do a proper trademark clearance search before adopting your name or tagline can save you a lot of money in design expenses incurred in re-branding! According to Steve Forbes "your brand is the single most important investment you can make in your business."

KEY TAKEAWAYS

- Your brand identity, including your business name, logo, and tagline are protectable intellectual property assets.
- You may use the ^{TM} and ^{SM} symbols even if you have not filed a trademark registration application.
- Filing for a trademark or service mark registration with the USPTO provides the strongest protection for brand identity assets.
- Your website content, blog posts, course material, ebooks, and books are protected automatically by copyright.
- Filing a copyright registration with the U.S. Copyright Office is required to legally pursue copyright infringement of your copyright assets.
- If timely filed, proactive registration of your copyright allows you to claim statutory damages and attorney fees.

8

SETTING SAIL

Twenty years from now, you will be more disappointed by the things you didn't
do than those you did. So throw off the bowlines. Sail away from safe harbor.
Catch the trade winds in your sails. Explore. Dream. Discover.
H. Jackson Brown, Jr. *(attributed to his mother)*

To recap everything you've just read, the five keys to launching a legally sound business include:

1. Creating a firm foundation for your business by registering a business entity.
2. Gathering a team of professionals to help you navigate areas outside your own skill set.
3. Using contracts to protect your business and mitigate legal risks.
4. Ensuring compliance with regulations through established policies and procedures.
5. Protecting your own Intellectual Property and doing the

research to ensure you are not infringing others' Intellectual Property rights.

Making sure these keys are in place positions your business for smooth sailing and a successful journey!

In conclusion I want to say, please don't allow the sometimes scary, consistently confusing, and occasionally overwhelming legal aspects of starting and running a small business to keep you from sharing your brilliance with the world. If you made it this far, you clearly have the desire to run your business in a legally sound way and I applaud you for taking the steps necessary to make that happen! I truly believe that the world needs your brilliance; it needs your light to shine brightly and guide the way for others who need what you uniquely have to share. Just as I hope you've found some small measure of guidance in what I have been able to share.

True, we [lawyers] build no bridges. We raise no towers. We construct no engines. We paint no pictures—unless as amateurs for our own principal amusement. There is little of all that we do which the eye of man can see. But we smooth out difficulties; we relieve stress; we correct mistakes; we take up other men's burdens and by our efforts we make possible the peaceful life of men in a peaceful state.

— JOHN WILLIAM DAVIS, AMERICAN
POLITICIAN, DIPLOMAT, AND LAWYER

TO PARAPHRASE THE ABOVE QUOTE BY JOHN DAVIS: THERE is little I do as an attorney that you can see with your eyes. What I strive to do is smooth out difficulties, relieve stress, correct mistakes, take up other small business owner's burdens and by my efforts provide them a peaceful life.

And, oh yeah, a compliant and legally protected business!

9

GLOSSARY

*T*his is a complete glossary of acronyms found within this book.

ADA: Americans with Disabilities Act is a civil rights law that prohibits discrimination against individuals with disabilities in areas including jobs, schools, transportation, and all places that are open to the general public.

CAN-SPAM: The CAN-SPAM Act is a United States federal law enforced by the FTC that provides rules for sending commercial email and messages, gives recipients the right to opt-out of receiving emails and messages, and sets penalties for violations.

CASL: Canada's Anti-Spam Law is the Canadian law counterpart to the United States CAN-SPAM Act.

CCPA: California Consumer Privacy Act is a California law that regulates the collection and use of personal information from California citizens.

CPRA: California Privacy Rights Act is a California law passed during the 2020 election cycle that provides broad privacy rights to California citizens, similar to the GDPR. The law will become effective January 1, 2023, with a lookback period to January 1, 2022.

CRM: Customer Relationship Management refers to software that enables you to track customer information and engagement.

DIY: Do It Yourself

DMCA: Digital Millennium Copyright Act is a United States federal copyright law that, in part, limits the liability of the providers of online services for copyright infringement by their users.

DPO: Data Protection Officer refers to a required resource under the GDPR for requesting changes to personal information or reporting violations.

EIN: The Employer Identification Number is an identifier from the IRS for your business, similar to a social security number, that is used for tax purposes.

FTC: The Federal Trade Commission is a United States federal agency that enforces anti-trust and unfair practices laws with the broad aim of maintaining consumer protection and prohibiting unfair competition in the economy.

GDPR: General Data Protection Regulations is a European Union law that regulates the collection, use, and protection of personal information obtained from European Union citizens.

IP: Intellectual Property refers to the body of creations protected by patent, copyright, and trademark laws including things such as inventions, literary and artistic works, and company names and logos used in commerce.

IRS: The Internal Revenue Service is a bureau of the United States Department of the Treasury responsible for collecting taxes and enforcing the federal tax laws.

NDA: Non-Disclosure Agreement is a type of contract that prevents the parties from sharing or disclosing information provided under the terms of the agreement.

OSHA: Occupational Safety and Health Administration – a bureau of the United States Department of Labor responsible for ensuring safe and healthful working conditions by setting and enforcing standards and by providing training, outreach, education and assistance.

QBO: QuickBooks Online is an online software program/app that allows you to track bookkeeping records and tax information for your business.

SBA: United States Small Business Administration is a cabinet-level federal agency dedicated to helping small business owners and entrepreneurs obtain counseling, capital, and contracting expertise.

U.S. Copyright Office: The United States Copyright Office, a division of the Library of Congress, is the federal agency responsible for approving and maintaining records of copyright registration in the United States including a Copyright Catalog.

USPTO: The United States Patent and Trademark Office is the United States federal agency responsible for granting U.S. patents and registering trademarks.

SMOOTH SAILING
BUSINESS CHECKLIST

*Y*ou may be surprised that setting up a website, email newsletter, printing brochures and business cards, and other activities aren't on this list. The truth is that you can launch your business without any of the marketing in place. That can be added as you go along and start earning income.

___ 1. Develop a business plan—determine your product or service, your target market, and your business model. How will you make money?

___ 2. Brainstorm a list of potential names for your business.

___ 3. Research your business name for availability. Make sure you have done a trademark clearance search BEFORE you register your business entity with your state.

___ 4. Choose a business entity based on your current and future plans.

___ 5. Register your business entity with your state. If you are going with sole proprietorship, but using any name other than your own, register a fictitious name. Otherwise, register for the appropriate entity using your chosen (and cleared) business name.

___ 6. Obtain an EIN from the IRS.

___ 7. Apply for any needed licenses and permits.

___ 8. Open a business bank account. Also, a business credit card and merchant account if needed. Remember to keep all business transactions separate from personal transactions.

___ 9. Bind your Business Insurance coverage, if needed.

___ 10. Create your Services Contract(s) (or if products, at least have a refund policy nailed down).

___ 11. Set up your bookkeeping systems. Whether electronic or paper, you want this ready to go. You've already incurred expenses for business registration, insurance, and the like—you want to be recording all of this as you go so you don't miss anything.

___ 12. Open for Business!

RESOURCES

*T*his list of resources will provide sustenance for your journey.

Association of Women's Business Centers: https://awbc.org/

Entrepreneur.com. Videos, webinars, franchise opportunities: https://www.entrepreneur.com/

Federal Trade Commission. Information and guidance on compliance with various regulations, establishing breach protocols, how to respond in the event of a data breach: https://www.ftc.gov

- Federal Trade Commission – data breach response guide - https://www.ftc.gov/tips-advice/business-center/guidance/data-breach-response-guide-business

- Federal Trade Commission – compliance guide for email marketing under the CAN-SPAM Act - https://www.ftc.gov/

tips-advice/business-center/guidance/can-spam-act-compliance-guide-business

Internal Revenue Service. Information and application to apply for an Employer Identification Number: https://www.irs.gov/businesses/small-businesses-self-employed/apply-for-an-employer-identification-number-ein-online

National Veteran Small Business Coalition: https://www.nvsbc.org/

Small Business Administration. General business information and videos, information about SBA loans and programs for small businesses: www.sba.gov

- Small Business Administration: business plan templates - https://www.sba.gov/business-guide/plan-your-business/write-your-business-plan

- To find SBA district and regional offices: https://www.sba.gov/about-sba/sba-locations

Small Business Development Centers. Find the small business development center near you. https://americassbdc.org/small-business-consulting-and-training/find-your-sbdc/

SCORE (Service Corps. of Retired Executives). Browse their library of articles and webinars or sign up for a mentor (it's free!) to help guide you in developing your business: https://www.score.org

The Tax and Legal Playbook—Second Edition by Mark J. Kohler, CPA & Attorney. Discusses small business tax strategies for maximizing income.

U.S. Copyright Office. Information on filing copyright applications: https://www.copyright.gov

- DMCA Instructions - www.copyright.gov/dmca-directory/transcripts/register.pdf

- Designate an Agent Instructions - www.copyright.gov/onlinesp/tutorials/transcripts/designate-an-agent.pdf

- Designate your agent: www.dmca.copyright.gov/login.html

U.S. Patent and Trademark Office. Watch a 42-minute video that walks you through basic trademark information. It will be useful to understand these basics before you consult with an attorney: https://www.uspto.gov/trademarks-getting-started/trademark-basics

ACKNOWLEDGMENTS

I would like to thank all of the awesome, powerful, courageous women (and a few men) who inspired and encouraged me during the difficult first year journey of transition from my long-term corporate identity to self-employed small business attorney to published author.

Lynne Williams and the Philadelphia Area Great Careers Group was my first networking group out of the gate and where I first learned the art of the 30 second introduction. Lynne is a fabulous connector and got me started down the networking path.

Kristen Zavo, who I first met through her LinkedIn profile challenge (great stuff!) and because I was so impressed with the value she delivered, signed up for her Job Joy business coaching. Kristen and my Job Joy classmates encouraged me when I was at my lowest point trying to figure out what my next chapter would be.

Jill Celeste and the Virtual Networkers was where I found my tribe and my very warm welcome into the world of entrepreneurship. The Virtual Networkers have been supporters, cheerleaders, and friends from my very first meeting.

All my sisters at Polka Dot Powerhouse, especially the Bensalem, King of Prussia, Lancaster, and Montgomeryville chapters, and The DivaGirl Tribe, headed by Majet Reyes and Tiffaney Whipple. Both groups offer me a truly fun and energetic group of powerful, authentic women.

My very special first year clients – you all know who you are – and know that because of attorney/client confidentiality I'm not going to name you here.

All my Advance Readers and Blurbers – and especially to Bob Hull who was the first person to tell me I could do this (and later was happy to tell me "I told you so").

My daughter, Sarah, my head cheerleader, the one who called me out when I was losing my grip, and whose candid observations have kept me on task and organized during this crazy year.

My husband, Jay, my first mate and staunch supporter of any float plan that steers us into financially abundant waters.

Finally, those that contributed directly to bringing this book to market: Suzanne T. Moore, my guide and mentor for all things marketing; Hanne Brøter, for keeping me on brand and visually conveying the message this book was meant to deliver; and last, but never least, Deborah Kevin and Highlander Press, for guiding me step-by-step through the process of becoming a published author, for telling me I had enough back when this book was barely sixty pages (and thereby lighting the fire under me to make it more), for believing in me and my vision, and most of all, for being my friend. Thank you doesn't begin to cover it.

ABOUT THE AUTHOR

Photo credit: Brenda Jankowski

Cheri D. Andrews, Esq., owns her own law practice, through which she helps small business owners and solopreneurs address the areas of their business—from corporate structure, contracts, and compliance, to copyright and trademark—where proper attention to the legal details will help them avoid costly mistakes and provide them the confidence of knowing that both THEY and their livelihood are legally protected! When she is not working, Cheri enjoys digital scrapbooking, mixed media art, reading, and travel. Cheri resides in Perkasie, Pennsylvania, with husband Jay of thirty-five years. She is the proud mother of three successful young adult daughters, and grandma to fur babies Millie and Nemo.

For more information, please visit:
www.cheriandrews.com,
or join her Facebook group, Let's Talk Legal:
www.facebook.com/groups/sbletstalklegal.

ABOUT THE PUBLISHER

Highlander Press, founded in 2019, is a hybrid publishing company committed to sharing big ideas and changing the world through words.

Highlander Press guides authors from where they are in the writing-editing-publishing process to where they have an impactful book of which they are proud, making a long-time dream come true. Having authored a book improves your confidence, helps create clarity, and ensures that you claim your expertise.

What makes Highlander Press unique is our business model focuses on building strong relationships and collaborating with women-owned businesses, which specialize in some aspect of the publishing industry, such as graphic design, book marketing, book launching, copyrights, and publicity. The mantra "a rising tide lifts all boats" is one we embrace.

BIBLIOGRAPHY

Girard, Scott L., Michael F. O'Keefe, and Marc A. Price. *Sales and Marketing: Learn What You Need in 2 Hours*. Herentals, Belgium: Nova Vista, 2014.

Hart, James W. *Business Law Basics: A Legal Handbook for Online Entrepreneurs and Start Up Businesses*. Amazon KDP, 2016.

Kohler, Mark J. *The Tax and Legal Playbook: Game-Changing Solutions to Your Small Business Questions*. Second Edition. Irvine, CA: Entrepreneur Press, 2015.

Pakroo, Peri. *The Small Business Start-Up Kit: A Step-By-Step Legal Guide*. 11th ed. NOLO, 2020.

Rees, Johnathan. *DO/PROTECT/Legal Advice for Startups*. London: The Do Book Company, 2014.

Steingold, Fred, and David Steingold. *Legal Guide for Starting & Running a Small Business*. 16th ed. NOLO Press, 2019.

ENDNOTES

[1] Affairs, Office of Consumer. "Canada's Anti-Spam Legislation - Home." Home - Canada's Anti-Spam Legislation. Innovation, Science and Economic Development Canada, April 21, 2020. https://fightspam.gc.ca/eic/site/030.nsf/eng/home.

[2] "FTC Publishes Inflation-Adjusted Civil Penalty Amounts." Federal Trade Commission, January 14, 2020. https://www.ftc.gov/news-events/press-releases/2020/01/ftc-publishes-inflation-adjusted-civil-penalty-amounts.